Partnerships
in Dental Practice

Sahalie Press
Woodinville, Washington

Books by Dr. Marc Cooper

Mastering the Business of Practice

Partnerships in Dental Practice

SOURCE: The Genesis of Success in Business and Life

Running on Empty:
Answers to Questions Dentists have about the Recession

PARTNERSHIPS IN DENTAL PRACTICE

Why Some Succeed and Why Some Fail

By

Marc B. Cooper, DDS, MSD

with

Thomas Ziegler, DDS, MS, JD
Art Haines, MS, CHE

PARTNERSHIP
Why Some Succeed and Why Some Fail

Published by Sahalie Press
Woodinville, Washington

ISBN: 978-0-9763584-2-8

Printed in the U.S.A.

Second Edition, 2009

Editing by Russell Jackson

WHY BUY THIS BOOK?

Because It Answers the Hard Questions

- Economically, dental partnerships make great sense in terms of optimizing assets, sharing costs, increasing revenues and fine-tuning division of labor. Yet in the United States, over 87% of dentists practice solo, and this has held steady for decades.

  What causes this overwhelming and enduring pattern of dentists continuing to practice solo?

- Top practice management advisers declare, "One sure way to realize a return on investment in your practice is to transition the practice from a solo to a partnered enterprise." They recommend the process of associateship to partnership, selling 50% to the partner, then continuing to work in the practice and selling the remaining 50% downstream.

  This works only if and when the partnership works. What do you do with an expanded practice if the partnership doesn't work?

- The majority of dental associateships and partnerships underperform or fail altogether. Although no clear studies are available, a number of dental journals report the failure rate in dental partnerships to be somewhere between 70% and 90%.

  Why do dental partnerships have such an extremely high morbidity rate?

- Nearly all associateships and partnerships begin with tremendous goodwill, excitement and enthusiasm. The future appears bright. However, it is not uncommon that within five years, the shine disappears and is replaced with dissatisfaction.

  What causes partnerships to unravel?

- When an associateship-to-partnership fails, the costs are extremely high in terms of money, time and emotional distress. The effect on staff performance and patient relations can be demoralizing as well.

  Partnership failure in dental practices costs hundreds of millions of dollars every year and untold emotional damage. What can be done to prevent this?

- Surveys reveal the majority of dentists have difficulty in communications, particularly with their associates or partners. Consequently, they are ineffective at handling problems directly, resolving conflicts and making mutual business decisions.

  What are the factors that thwart a dentist's ability to effectively communicate to an associate or partner?

It seems dentists are in a quandary. A clear path to economic freedom and asset optimization exists through recruiting an associate and transitioning the associate to a partner. The problem is most dental partnerships don't work.

This book provides answers to the most common and destructive issues and problems that cause dental partnerships to fail. If you are considering a partnership as a strategy, or if you currently have an associate or partner, this book will enhance your ability to succeed.

Dr. Marc B. Cooper
The Mastery Company

THE MASTERY PROMISE

*"Mastering your enemies makes you strong.
Mastering yourself makes you fearless."
~ Lao Tzu*

In consulting a new client, my first step is to establish a clear definition of what it means to be successful. How would success look? How would it feel? How would you measure success? Who would you be that you're not now being if you were successful?

My personal definition of success in writing this book begins and ends with its impact on you. I'll consider it a triumph if it opens your eyes, engages your awareness and expands your understanding of yourself as an owner, manager, leader and marketer.

This was never intended to be a How-To book. This is a Who-To book. This volume is a mirror, in a way. Hold it up, look directly into your own eyes and fearlessly examine yourself and how you are running your practice as a business.

This book is presented in question and answer format. The questions come from clients and other dentists around the country. I selected each question in this book because I've run into it numerous times in more than two decades as a practice management consultant. They are questions I know you ask yourself – nearly every day.

My promise is a book that is eye-opening and energetic – one that will be ragged at the edges in five years. A book that impacts the way you run your practice as a business. A book true to the Mastery spirit and to those seeking to master the business of their practice. You have now taken the first step in your commitment to success.

Be fearless.

Marc B. Cooper, DDS, MSD

INTRODUCTION

As soon as I graduated from orthodontic school, I began looking for a partner. I was not interested in buying someone out or starting my own practice, I was interested in a true partnership – although at the time I did not understand what that meant.

One of the orthodontists in town, Dr. John Lohse, showed interest, and, after some very preliminary conversations, asked me to join him on a conference call with Dr. Marc Cooper. During that call, Marc asked John and me to write down, in document form, to be given to each other and to become part of our contract, the three following things: our "core values," our "conditions of satisfaction" and our "goals for ourselves and our practice for the next one, three and five years."

I had no clue what he was talking about. He was not speaking any language I had heard before. But after some explanation from Marc and further explanation from my partner-to-be, I began to see what Marc was intent on accomplishing. He was setting up a platform on which to build a partnership, a partnership that would start with open communication and a partnership that had each party's expectations out on the table. I then understood who Marc was – he was a mentor and coach for partnerships.

Marc taught me in his new language that "unfulfilled expectations lead to upset." In my mind, I saw what I thought a partnership should look and act and feel like. And in my future partner's mind, he saw what he thought a partnership should look and act and feel like. Those were our expectations. If the partnership did not turn out that way, it would lead to upset. And if that upset wasn't managed properly or in a timely matter, the partnership was doomed to fail. In my view, that is one reason – if not the main reason – most partnerships fail.

John and I have now had a successful partnership for 12 years -- and we have added another partner. Don't get me wrong, we have had our share of breakdowns. But we've learned that, as Marc puts it, "well-managed breakdowns lead to breakthroughs." Marc has taught us that if we declare that we have a breakdown, we can move a conversation from "blame and fault" to a conversation of "future and solution." That type of conversation forces both parties to stop what has been causing the breakdown or problem – and starts the partners on a path to a solution for that problem. It actually is fairly easy once you realize what you are doing – and then manage it. Unfortunately, so often we are so immersed in our breakdowns that we need someone from the outside, a coach like Marc, to step in.

When I became a partner, our practice had 10 staff members. We now have 28 full-time staff members. When you have fewer than 10 – say, six or seven – you can manage by "relationship." When you have more, managing by relationship is no longer effective. Breakdowns start to occur and growth is hindered. Marc has coached us through our extreme growth by first helping us set up a management team with team leaders. When growth took us beyond the effectiveness of a management team alone, Marc helped us understand how professional help in the form of a senior management team could get us to the next level. Our senior management team includes these seasoned professionals: a CPA/MBA person, a human resources person, a marketing person, our business manager and the three doctors.

Next, Marc guided us to the next stage, so now we are functioning as a corporate enterprise. We have recently set up an operating Board of Directors to take us to yet another level of professionalism, all with the coaching, encouragement and sometimes the dragging of Marc. We are learning to govern the enterprise. And we are creating a company where policy governs, not people.

With Marc as your coach, you will hear a lot about "future." I have learned through the teachings of Marc – and then have had it driven home through experience – that if your future is used up, breakdowns will increase tenfold. Marc taught us that if you are not working on "what's next," you have used up your future and things will start to fall apart. Marc is constantly asking us what our one-, three- and five-year goals are and how we will take our practice to the next level. If we do not have good answers to those questions, he will tell us to get on the ball and create our next future.

It has been amazing to me over the past 12 years how many times one of my colleagues has come up to me and told me that he or she is thinking about bringing on a partner and wants to know what transition company we used to set up the deal. He or she usually goes on to explain that it is obvious that we have a great partnership and that we must have used a great company to put together the perfect contract.

I proceed to tell them that, yes, the company we used did do a great job and that the contract does need to be well-written. But then I talk about a consultant who acts like a mentor and coach – more like a partnership counselor. I tell whoever asks that long before the transition company was involved, this consultant was working with us to determine if our goals and core values were a match, if our conditions of satisfaction could be met and if we were partnership material. I explain how expectations, if not met, will lead to failure. I talk with great passion about how the true secret of our success does not lie in the contract, but in the work we did with Marc and the work we continue to do with Marc. I tell people – and I would tell all who read this – that I could not even begin to imagine trying to have a successful partnership without the help of Dr. Marc Cooper.

All I can say is, "Thank you, Marc."

Brent R. Corbridge DMD, MSD
Orthodontic Partners
Reno, Nevada

FOREWORD

When asked to write a foreword for this book on Partnership, I questioned if our partnership story had any special significance compared to others. After all, everyone has probably experienced similar trials and tribulations in their partnerships, but perhaps that's just the point. Our story isn't really unique, and perhaps others are experiencing the same problems that we have faced.

After reading this book, I can honestly say the material in it reflects our own experience and our partnership story. Each page holds the same issues and breakdowns we encountered. The responses to the questions posed in this book are basically the same we received. And most important, when we followed Marc's advice, we were able to effectively handle our partnership concerns and problems.

Our story began with a friendship that started in dental school. Shortly after graduating, Randy (my partner) and I found ourselves owning separate general dental practices in South Lake Tahoe, California. Ten years went by and Randy made the decision to sell his practice and return to graduate school to specialize in endodontics.

Because of our friendship and common interests in endodontics, I suddenly found my self dreaming of a future endodontic partnership. Two years following his decision, my practice was for sale and I was accepted to the same residency program at Boston University. Our early partnership vision was that Randy would return to the West, locating in Reno, Nevada, and wait until my residency commitment was complete. During the two years I was in Boston, we discussed plans for our practice, selected a location and developed plans for our space.

Randy and I felt as though we saw the world the same way. What could be better than two people who had attended the same undergraduate program, practiced dentistry in the same town for many years, attended the same graduate program, enjoyed similar sports and the same philosophical values and were good friends as well? I actually remember Randy telling a new employee, "Dave and I are exactly alike."

After opening the doors of our practice, the differences between us begin to appear almost immediately. We interacted very differently with our staff members. Randy wanted to be loved by everyone. I felt like I had to be the general, to keep the troops in line. We had different views on how we should interact with patients. We had different views on managing conflict and problems. What I thought was a problem, Randy felt would probably just go away with enough time. Decision-making was laborious and often resulted in procrastination. We began to realize that we were two very different people. All these things, of course, caused problems and stress between us. This was not the result we had envisioned for our partnership.

Then we stumbled upon Dr. Cooper. Actually it wasn't a stumble at all. We had been referred to Marc by a respected colleague. I was reluctant to initiate a contract with Marc, as I have been involved with many different well-known and nationally recognized management gurus and programs over the years. These experiences usually led to a rehash of developing operational systems and polices. We did not want some cookbook course, with a manual of written job descriptions and policies. We wanted a real business and partnership coach. This person would need to be actively involved in the development our talents and skills to resolve the fundamental issues of our partnership.

Our first conversation with Marc was a discussion about language. Now, that got our attention! It wasn't about how much we produced and regurgitating budget numbers. He explained that partnerships usually break down because expectations have not been put out in the open and discussed. Randy and I had expectations of each other that were not being met. I thought Randy should see the world as I did. Randy couldn't understand why I didn't see the world as he did. These differences in expectations usually bubbled up in the form of an upset between us. Marc started by asking us what we felt we needed to work on. This was a much different approach than my past management consultant experiences. Our partnership was the primary issue, and that is where we started.

Marc began working with us to establish consistent communication. He brought ideas and language tools to our coaching sessions that promoted effective communication. We began scheduling monthly partnership meetings. We developed an agenda that asked such questions as: "Are there any expectations you have of me that I am not fulfilling? What could I be doing better? Do you have any requests of me?" Wow! We never had such uncomfortable honest dialogue.

We began understanding each other, learned how to make requests and got that these requests needed mutual agreement and conditions of satisfaction for their fulfillment. This process greatly strengthened our partnership as we began generating a dialogue about us, and not just about the operational problems of the business.

Marc helped us understand that we had used up our future. We had achieved all of our initial development and growth objectives and had no more future. Marc coached us in the development of a strategic plan with written goals and objectives for our newly created future. We developed a one-, three- and five-year plan with specific targets so that we could measure our results. Part of our strategic plan called for the development of a management team.

We had never thought that our small office needed different levels of management. However, we proceeded to develop an executive committee involving key staff members that demonstrated management capabilities. This made a significant difference in reducing stress in the practice. It allowed involvement and ownership for the staff, and clarified reporting relationships and delegation of authority. One of the great benefits of creating a management team is that it allowed Randy and me to practice endodontics without being bombarded with management decisions throughout the day.

Marc then started introducing the idea of governance for the partnership. We didn't have any idea of what this really meant, but everything else Marc had suggested seemed to be working, so why not? We then began working through a partnership governance program. We developed policies that would direct us in making decisions and establish protocol for functioning as a Board of Directors (just like a real business). This was an exciting process! It truly defines what the partners expect as stakeholders of the practice and what benefits the practice will provide for the owners. It also lays out expectations, roles and conditions of satisfaction for future associates and partners.

Randy and I still have times when we don't communicate very well. We still experience breakdowns and conflicts. The difference is we have a committed future now. We are educated and have a new language that allows us to manage these breakdowns and move to action in resolving them. We have plans to expand our practice in the near future. This is an exciting place to be. What we can now offer a new associate or partner is a far cry from what we had previous to Marc's coaching.

Marc is the real deal. He has a unique talent to see through the smoke screens and deal with the important issues in a partnership.

He brings skills honed in the corporate world that I feel are unmatched in coaching dental partnerships today.

This book definitely reflects the coaching Marc gave us. What you can't get from the book is the kind of relationship Marc has with us. You can't feel his piercing intention, his rigorous driving commitment, his no-nonsense way of getting you and your partner to perform at the highest level possible. But if you are in a partnership or associateship, or even thinking about it, read this book. It will give you invaluable information on how to have a successful partnership.

David M. Reeves DDS, CAGS
David M. Reeves DDS and Randall J. Iwasiuk DDS Ltd.
Reno, Nevada

ACKNOWLEDGEMENTS

I hold my clients as my business partners. They in turn hold me as a committed partner to their success – not just as an expert, coach or adviser. Being this kind of partner with my clients is one thing that differentiates me.

My clients have someone fully committed to their success as an owner, as a leader and as a manager. As their partner, I am charged with providing them with education, training and coaching that enables them to produce remarkable business results. What this partnership with my clients does for me is push me to deliver and coach at the very highest level, allowing me to generate peak performance in myself. A true win-win.

An authentic partnership is a special kind of relationship. Partners have full permission to hold each other accountable. Partners empower each other's performance. Partners talk straight to each other. Partners share an unconditional commitment to each other's success. Inside a partnership, inside a real partner relationship, both parties are enabled to perform at their highest level, producing extraordinary results – much greater than they could ever do alone.

I also work with some extraordinary collaborative consulting partners, top-of-the-rank consultants in their own right, two of whom contributed to this book. These collaborative partners provide advice and counsel to my clients in areas of business, corporate structure and processes. Every dental partnership needs to manage its liabilities, manage its downside risk, pre-empt common legal issues and markedly increase its performance as a business.

My experience of coaching hundreds of associateships and partnerships over the last 20 years and my learning from my clients and our collaborative advisers have given me "deep smarts" about what makes partnerships fail and what makes them succeed. So I want to acknowledge my clients and collaborative consultants who have contributed so much to my knowledge and my coaching.

Special thanks to Dr. Tom Ziegler and Mr. Art Haines for contributing their experience and expertise to this book. And a very special thanks to Chris Creamer, my long-time business partner and friend, who consistently enables me to bring my visions into reality.

Dr. Marc B. Cooper DDS, MSD
MasteryCompamy.com

DISCLAIMER

Results are a function of integrity and structure.

The information in this book can inform, coach and teach, but it cannot do it for you.

The information in this book cannot force you to operate with integrity.

The information in this book cannot give you the courage to confront problems with your partner or associate.

The information in this book cannot make you build and manage your structures.

It is up to you. You are responsible.

By responsibility, I mean that you see yourself as "cause in the matter."

Blame, shame, guilt and fault are the antithesis of responsibility.

No problem can be solved, no issue effectively handled, no concern effectively addressed, unless you hold that you are responsible.

Integrity is honoring your word as yourself.

Integrity is making and keeping promises.

Integrity is holding yourself, each staff member and the practice accountable for its word.

So as you read this book and gain new knowledge and insights into your practice and yourself, remember: It is up to you to implement what you learn.

CONTENT

INTRODUCTION TO PARTNERSHIP

The benefits of partnership in dentistry are easily recognized. A dentist can realize dramatic increases in asset value or share or unit price of the practice. With a partner, a dentist can significantly increase revenues, margin and cash flow, while at the same time decreasing work load, management time, emergency coverage and stress of ownership. But the costs of a failed partnership are also tremendous – significant loss of money, time, well being, patients and staff.

Many partnerships fail. What are the primary causes for these failures? How do you manage the issues or concerns that cause them? These are the questions which I have been grappling with for more than 20 years.

We have spent a lot of time analyzing American Dental Association survey data from many years back, trying to extract meaningful information about partnerships in private practice. Neither the ADA nor any other agency or company directly measures this domain of partnerships in any depth. So we were left to circuitously interpret information from various data sets.

What the ADA surveys indicate is a very minor increase in dental partnerships during the years we've been examining. According to the data, the incidence of partnerships in dentistry went from 12.9% in 1999 to 13.6% in 2002. Basically, the same slight increase occurred in employed dentists (associates are part of this mix), which climbed slightly from 5.2% to 5.6% of practitioners.

Yet, if we take the claims of the major and lesser-known consulting companies, *Dental Economics* and practice management articles about how many partnerships are being formed, there are many more partnerships being formed than ever before. But if the number of overall partnerships is staying "flat," it can only mean many more partnerships are failing. Our conclusion is that dental associateships and partnerships are failing at a staggering rate.

Although "transitions" is the buzz, the issues I deal with in my work with clients primarily occur after the partnerships are formed and operational. It is not uncommon for a partnership to bring me in to work out the dissolution of their arrangement.

All partnerships need work. There is no way around it. Yet, most dental partners do little work on the partnership. It's like never servicing your car: It is bound to breakdown some day. Most dentists think after they have been through the formation process – Letter of Intent, Appraisal, Employment Agreement and/or Associate Agreement, Purchase Agreement, edit of Corporate Documents – they are basically done. In my view, the work is just beginning.

You CAN set up partnerships to win. You CAN structure and manage partnerships to stay out of trouble. You CAN set up partnerships to generate much greater success than solo practice. And that's what this book is about.

THE PROBLEM WITH PARTNERSHIPS IS THEY COME WITH PROBLEMS

Typical Scenario: Dr. Jones is very busy after 10 years or so in practice. He attends a seminar on transitions. Some of his buddies are in the midst of doing it themselves.

Dr. Jones becomes totally enrolled in following the path of recruiting an associate and converting that associate into a partner. He sees this path as "the answer."

What Dr. Jones cannot see is that this simple solution can just as easily turn into a bigger problem.

In this case, his problem is he is too busy. He's booked out six to eight weeks, the practice can't continue to grow and the competition is increasing. The solution? Get a partner. But what he may be blind to is this particular solution has intrinsic and possibly catastrophic risks.

Partnerships always – and I mean always – come with their own set of problems. Knowing that a partnership inherently has problems, the smart thing to do would be to pre-empt these problems and have structures and processes in place to address them before they cause real damage.

In addition to getting strong legal and business advice on how to structure the transactions and formulate the documents, focus the same kind of intention and attention on setting up and managing the partnership relationship and communication. If Dr. Jones fails to effectively set up the relationship and communication, the partnership will invariably fall into disarray or disorder.

This book is designed to give dentists, advisers and key staff members the knowledge, insights and governing structures to enable partners to address and manage the inevitable problems that arise in any partnership.

CAN YOU PASS THE PARTNERSHIP QUIZ?

I am a periodontist and I've been in practice for 22 years. I just attended a program on transitions and I liked what I heard. I definitely saw a way to optimize the asset value of my practice. My revenues are at a level ($1.32 million) where I could take the recommended actions to make a transition happen.

If I follow their formula, I pump-up the practice by working extra hard for 18 months. Then bring in an associate/partner and slow my pace down, keeping 50% of the practice to sell later.

It all sounds so good, but a nagging voice is telling me to be very cautious.

I'm really in a quandary about this whole thing. Where do I get valid information on partnerships? And how do I decide?

○   ○   ○

Partnerships have tremendous advantages when they succeed. But they have horrific costs when they fail. Given this dynamic, and given the high estimated failure rate of partnerships, you'd think there would be lots of research, case studies and valid statistics on what makes partnerships work. But there is very little data or information written on the subject of partnerships.

If the high failure rate we estimate is accurate, the costs of failure would have to run in the hundreds of millions of dollars. It's hard to understand why information on successful and failed partnerships is nowhere to be found. It's difficult to fathom why the ADA, which has had its own survey group for nearly 20 years and does yearly surveys of thousands of dentists, has yet to examine the success and failure of associateships or partnerships.

I wouldn't count on consulting enterprises that sell "transitions" to measure and report failures in associateships and partnerships. Why should they? Dentists are buying their services without any evidence. Dentists aren't asking the one essential question: "Of the deals you have put together, what is your rate of failed partnerships at three, five and 10 years?"

There is no hard evidence, no real valid information and no unbiased data about what works and what doesn't in generating a successful partnership. None. Zero. Zip. In my research, I haven't found one business school or post-graduate dental course on generating a successful partnership relationship – not one. Maybe that's why our consulting company has developed and now offers programs on how to generate and maintain a successful partnership. Maybe that's why our survey company developed a survey to measure success and failure in associateships and partnerships. These things are clearly needed.

Let me suggest you begin by taking the following Partnership Quiz as your first step. These are all Yes-No questions.

1. I know without a doubt I need a partner.
   [ ] Yes   [ ] No

2. Having a partner will make my life easier than practicing alone.
   [ ] Yes   [ ] No

3. I won't need to spend a lot of time and energy in selecting a partner.
   [ ] Yes   [ ] No

4. I fully believe that legal documents will keep me out of trouble.
   [ ] Yes   [ ] No

5. I know I will be afraid to directly confront my partner or cause a conflict.
    [ ] Yes   [ ] No

6. I am a "my way or the highway" kind of practice-owner.
    [ ] Yes   [ ] No

7. I know I will not be completely straight with my partner.
    [ ] Yes   [ ] No

8. Even if the partner candidate doesn't feel like a perfect fit, I know I can make it work anyway.
    [ ] Yes   [ ] No

9. I know I will be afraid to ask my partner for what I want.
    [ ] Yes   [ ] No

10. I must first be concerned with my own future, then my partner's success and well-being.
    [ ] Yes   [ ] No

11. I don't need to explore all the alternative possibilities – such as associates, employee dentists or independent contractors -- before I consider adding a partner.
    [ ] Yes   [ ] No

12. I believe what consultants say about partnerships: *They won't be a problem and you'll make more money!*
    [ ] Yes   [ ] No

If you answered 'Yes' to more than two of the questions above, I recommend that you NOT consider a partnership at this time.

Don't be fooled: Partnerships take hard work, commitment and structure to stay healthy. There is a far greater chance of their failing than succeeding without consistent attention and intention. Without clear and consistent structures and processes, the chances are better than not that a partnership will go down the toilet.

The upside potential for partnerships is incredible. But for all their upside potential, you need to understand that a partnership will complicate your life, not make it easier. Partnerships increase the risks. Sure it would be great to share the burdens and responsibilities. Sure it would be fabulous to find someone who has strengths where you have weaknesses. Yes, it would be great to have the advantages that partnership provides you for opening up new opportunities. Yes, it would be tremendous to have a comrade in arms at the top, where synergy and better decisions could be made.

Believe me, I understand and really appreciate the advantages of partnerships. When they work, they are fabulous. I have witnessed partnerships producing remarkable results. But I have also directly experienced the pain and the costs when they don't work.

Take the quiz!

IT IS DECISIVE

I am in the middle of dissolving my partnership of 11 years. The breakup is painful and expensive and it's really eating at me. I am bitter and want revenge – which is really unlike me. I am angry a lot of the time. The staff is freaking out. My production, collections and new patients are all suffering.

My partner and I are barely talking to each other. Right now, we have our attorneys working things out. The non-compete, what do we do with existing patients, staff, equipment, supplies and receivables are all points of disagreement. Although we had the terms of how to dissolve the partnership in the initial contract, it seems that after 11 years not much applies.

My partnership started out great. It worked really well for a long time. We both made money, we both grew our practices and we both became much better clinicians. I am not sure what we could have done to keep the partnership healthy.

What did I do wrong? Why do so many dental partnerships fail?

o   o   o

This is a multifaceted issue. There are numbers of elements required to keep a partnership healthy – relationship, vision, core values, mission and communication are but a few. Then there are various structures, systems and processes that ought to be instituted on a routine basis that ensure the partnership keeps working. But there is one overarching factor that is superior to all others that produces successful partnerships, and that is "context."

Two things you should know about context. One, it is difficult to talk about because it is not the way you ordinarily think about things.

And two, context is decisive. (Reference: *Discovering the Future* by Joel Barker)

First, given the high rate of partnership failure in dentistry, you need to realize there isn't something wrong with you as an individual. You don't have a character flaw. You aren't bad or stupid. Neither you nor your partner is directly at fault. Don't take on guilt or shame. Stop blaming yourself or your partner. And for heaven's sake, don't be a victim. Most partnerships in dentistry are like fish out of water: They survive only for a short period of time. And context is like water to the fish.

The context in which dentists are trained and practice is much more dominant in determining a successful partnership than the dentists' psychology, personality profile or even their daily actions.

The first level of context you grow up into is one I call *Dependent*. You depend on others for your existence. Within this context of *Dependent* there is no responsibility. You have no core values and the future you envision is pure fantasy. There is little separation of you from others.

But as you grow older, you move into the next context, *Independent*. You move from *Dependent* to *Independent* by defining yourself – by developing an identity – an "I."

In the context of *Independent*, the language used and the actions and thinking that work within it are "I, me, my." And this context of *Independent* is the principal context of dentistry today. Go to any dental meeting or study club and listen to how dentists talk about their practices. What you will hear is "my" practice. How "I" deliver care. Unfortunately, partnerships have a very hard time surviving within this context of "I, me, my."

On the high end of this context of *Independent,* you develop clear core values, you are responsible for yourself, you can give and keep your word and you can generate a very successful solo practice. But the futures that are available within this context are identity-based – because, ultimately, within this context you are engaged with "What's in it for me?" And "What's in it for me" is antithetical to creating a successful partnership.

There is a context that *Independent* can unfold into that I'll call *Interdependent*. The language that is used within this context is "we, us, our." This context is very uncommon in dentistry, but it is the context in which partnerships thrive.

A partnership within an *Independent* context is two individuals trying to satisfy two "I, me, mys" from one practice. Therefore, the practice often gets pulled in two distinct directions. A practice can't satisfy two "Is" at the same time. It's tough to serve two masters. Evidence for my assertion is the 80% to 90% failure rate of partnerships, the 99% failure rate of MSOs and the fact that 80% to 90% of dentists practice solo.

A partnership has a much greater chance of success within an *Interdependent* context. The practice has a single source to satisfy. Problems, futures, management, leadership, planning – all are different in this context because they only have to satisfy one master: one "us," not two "mes."

So most partnerships fail in dentistry because the context is *Independent* and not *Interdependent*. In this context, partnerships are hard pressed to survive. Can you generate this context of *Interdependent*? Yes. But in my experience, it takes education, training and development.

The definition of a partner is someone willing to share the other's downside risks, be committed to his or her success and well-being and share mutually agreed upon core values, fundamental beliefs and vision. Generating and maintaining a partnership relationship takes constant work and communication, with defined structures, systems and accountabilities. I'm willing to bet that your partnership had none of these in place. But even if you had these "structures, systems and accountabilities" in place, but didn't have the *context*, the partnership was destined to struggle, at best, or fail as yours has.

THE PERILS OF PARTNERSHIP

I have heard about your success with partnerships and the Mastery program. I am not in the Mastery program. I have been in practice 26 years. Four years ago, I signed a partnership agreement. "John" bought 50% of my practice with the right of first refusal for the other 50%. I am holding the note for the remainder of his buy-out. He put 20% down. He is purchasing 50% over a five-year period so the money can come out of his cash flow because he started with a debt of $200K, primarily from dental school. The partnership started out great, but now isn't working for me.

Before John, I had two other associates. John started out fabulous and looked like he'd be a tremendous asset to the practice. Everyone liked him – staff, patients and colleagues. Great clinical skills. Willing to learn. And he was OK with the "deal" and the money.

The first two to three years with John went pretty well. He got up to speed clinically. Started selling the bigger cases. But after that, I didn't see him continue his growth. It was like he went into cruise control. I didn't see him taking on more ownership and responsibility. John now takes more time off than that I do, which makes me mad. I think he should spend a lot more time at the practice. He takes more vacation time than I would have in his position. He's not very demanding on staff. And when it comes to marketing, he doesn't. What I wanted was someone who would step up as a leader. Someone who would really take the management load off of me. Someone who would actively market the practice. That's not what I have. Actually I am working harder than ever – still managing the staff, still pushing the numbers, still making it happen.

I feel stuck, frustrated and angry. What should I do now?

○   ○   ○

There are numerous pieces to this answer.

The very first piece is you. Yup – you! You know, the one in the mirror.

In my world, I hold that people are responsible. By responsible, I mean you see yourself as cause in the matter. If you ever worked with me, you would know that's how I operate. "You" would need to hold yourself as cause (source, origin, basis) for why things look and operate the way they do – and that would include your partnership. As you angrily point a finger at John, remember there are three pointing back at you. When you hold yourself responsible, you will begin to see these partnership issues as your own doing.

If I interviewed you, what I would hear from you is blame and fault about your partner's performance and attitude. Fault and blame are the antithesis of responsibility. Fault and blame are always about someone else doing it to you.

As we continued the interview, I would hear lots of assessments, judgments, evaluations, justifications and explanations – an entire soap opera – about your partner that would make you "right" and him "wrong." Then you'd sprinkle in your own personal statements, a number of "shoulds" and "should nots," making you even more right. The question now is: Would you rather be right or happy?

So the first step is taking a hard, honest look at how and what you did and didn't do to have the partnership not succeed. Confront WHY you did it and WHAT you got out of it. In my view, you can't move forward without this first step. The first step to resolving any problem is to take responsibility for it. If you are willing to do that, then we can take the next steps and have them work. But this step, the first step – to become responsible – is the most difficult, and the most necessary.

In my consulting and coaching work with partnership, that's where I begin. Once both partners authentically look at their responsibility in the matter, then, and only then, do we go forward.

Once each partner is willing to be responsible, then we go through a proven process:

- Aligning core values;

- Generating a strategic plan (vision, budgets, strategic analysis, performance goals and targets);

- Identifying strengths and weaknesses;

- Setting up conditions of satisfaction to allow each partner to share the downside risk;

- Identifying individual partnership accountabilities and setting up structures of fulfillment of these accountabilities;

- Generating a formal partnership set of agreements geared to "govern" the enterprise (policy should govern, not people); and

- Working on how to handle difficult and crucial conversations.

All that takes at least a year of hard work, and then I offer ongoing coaching to make sure the partnership delivers high performance and stays healthy. That's how I do it. I am sure there are other folks out there with their own methods, but this works for me and the people with whom I work. But it all begins and ends with your willingness to be responsible.

For me, an area that is clearly missing in the domain of transitions is that dentists and their advisers fail to directly confront the obvious, staring-you-right-in-the-face issue. Dentists have neither the background, the makeup, the skill sets nor the personalities to naturally form and manage successful partnerships. Heck, if they did, there would be a lot of them, and many more group practices and MSOs would have succeeded. Yet, without partnerships, the asset value of their dental practice will be diminished, not optimized.

My job is to first point out that the "emperor has no clothes" and then help the emperor figure out his wardrobe.

TRANSITION WORRIES

I am a 54-year-old general practitioner. I will do between $835K and $875K this year. The practice is growing about 4% a year. I have a staff of six, do mostly adult dentistry, more than 60% crown and bridge, with four days of hygiene a week. Question is: What's next?

I have attended transition seminars from a variety of vendors. They make it sound like a cake walk. But the horror stories about failed associateships and partnerships has me leery.

Question: What should I be thinking and doing now?

○   ○   ○

You have good reason to be apprehensive. The track record for dental partnerships is grim, with perhaps as much as an 80% failure rate. This failure rate is certainly in part due to poor structures and sequencing of events – such as Letters of Intent, Employment Agreements, Associate Agreements, Appraisals and Purchase Agreements. Everything these consulting groups and seminars are addressing. These are essential, critical and fundamental units to produce a well-designed and fairly financed package.

But from my view, the materials and processes to generate these documents are by far the least important reasons why dental partnerships fail.

Dental partnerships fail because dentists don't know how to be good partners.

In business and in life, it is all about relationship. There is a reason why 90% of dentists practice solo. There is a reason why most dentists have a hierarchical management structure. There is a reason why MSOs and DPMCs failed miserably in the 90s. And that reason is dentists are pretty lame at generating powerful partnership relations with others.

In our consulting work, we do a fair amount of personality profiling. We use the Enneagram, the Now, Discover Your Strengths Assessment and our own Mastery Dentist Satisfaction Survey, Associate Performance Survey and Dentist Performance Assessment. These assessments continue to demonstrate that dentists would much prefer to do nothing more than sit chair-side and work on patients. They also clearly demonstrate that dentists have a difficult time working with and for others.

So if you know your weakness going in – generating and maintaining strong partnership relationships – you at least understand that you need advice, counsel and some outside management to make a partnership work. And if you know this going in, if you recognize that to make it work you need outside help in this area, then you'll seek and find people to assist you in being successful in generating and maintaining your partnership.

I have a model, a program and a management structure for dentists that produce successful partnerships. I am very proud to say that I have a 90% success rate over the last 10 years. I am surprised (and also delighted) that no one in the industry comes even close to this success rate in partnership relations.

How do I do it? I understand the principle *"Win, then play."* I understand the barriers and inherent faults in generating and sustaining a healthy partnership. I know how to coach people to make it work. I work intensively with the senior dentist and the incoming dentist to set up their relationship based on several proven core elements, teach them how to communicate effectively with each other, work with them to learn how to confront issues immediately and resolve them and assist them in setting up an ongoing structure to manage and maintain a healthy, productive partnership relationship. And my results continue to support the assertion that my method works.

It isn't that you should not follow the path of transitions. No, you should. But you need to first come to grips with the fact that you'll need work and support in developing and managing your relationship with your future partner – because the odds are quite high that by yourself you don't have the tools on your own to structure and manage a successful partnership.

WHY PARTNERSHIPS FAIL

I have been in a partnership for eight years. We have both done really well. But now we have a number of issues that are driving me to seriously consider breaking up the partnership.

The issues are primarily around purchasing a building. We are so far apart on many points in this transaction that I don't think we can resolve our differences. And I am not sure I even want to.

What's happening is all the things that I have been tolerating in him up until now are becoming intolerable. I find myself upset all the time. I keep getting angry when I think about how little he thinks about what I contribute to the practice or his stubbornness in these negotiations.

I feel stuck and upset. Neither of us is talking about it directly. We pretend everything is OK, but I think both of us are seething underneath.

I have already put a call into my attorney. My wife wants me to do something ASAP because I am always upset and complaining. It's just a big mess!

What should I do?

o   o   o

This is good question. A significant portion of our work over the last decade has been dealing with dental partnerships. Our track record is one of the best in the business.

Although there are a number of *transition* gurus who'll handle the Appraisal, Letter of Intent, Employee Agreement, Purchase Agreement and even the financing – beware! These factors rarely, if ever, are the primary cause of partnerships failing. The reason partnerships fail is not because documents and plans are not well done. They don't fail because the model used for the purchase of assets and good will is flawed. No, they fail because of the inability of the partners to communicate.

It's been reported that 80%-plus of dental associateship-to-partnerships fail in the first five years. And 50% of those that make it to partnership fail in the next five years – a pretty dismal statistic about dentists and their ability to generate successful partnerships. (I wonder what the total amount of money that's lost in these failures is. It must be in the hundreds of millions.)

My first piece of coaching is that you and your partner get and read the book *Difficult Conversations* by Stone, Patton and Heen. You and your partner clearly have never mastered the ability to have straight, no-nonsense, honest, effective communications with each other.

My next piece of coaching is the following 10 Cardinal Rules for Managing Breakdowns with your Partner.

RULE 1

Never lose your temper. Don't let anything become personal. Loss of emotional control will lead you to say and do things in the name of anger that will come back to haunt you later. Resist the urge to argue or verbally abuse your partner.

RULE 2

Do not gossip with any of your staff. Not even that staff member with whom you are closest – the one who has always been your ally. No one! Don't try to get agreement, sympathy or support for your point of view about your partner from any staff member. Once the staff senses the partnership is in trouble, they'll start to take sides and look for their next job, and their performance will start to go down the toilet.

RULE 3

Be very clear on this: It is not important that you get along in a "kumbaya" sort of way. Get along to achieve. Keep your eyes on the collective prize. It's very simple – partnerships produce a much better margin than solo practices. You make more money and it costs you less to practice if you sustain the partnership. It's not a marriage, it's a business relationship.

RULE 4

Stay focused on the mission. When you have a common mission, you can overcome differences. You don't need to get along when you focus on winning. If you never had a mission, if you never had a common vision, if you never aligned on your core values – you are missing a major cornerstone of partnership. Tough to put them in when the building is already constructed, but it can be done.

RULE 5

You need to understand each other in order to get over your differences. Again, both of you get and read *Difficult Conversations* and follow their model. It works!

RULE 6

Don't fall into "I can't stand you." Not liking each other may be the way it is, but "I can't stand you" is a choice. When you can't stand someone, you obsess. When you obsess, you have a flurry of negative thoughts about the other person that cause you to be upset and dramatically enlarge your partner's weaknesses. When you obsess, yesterday holds tomorrow hostage so you lose the future. Keep yourself and your partner focused on the vision, mission, goals and projects at hand.

RULE 7

You need to separate the issues from the person. Don't blame him, fault him or try to shame him. Don't use "you" statements. Keep the relationship at a professional level. Learn how to have a dialogue rather than a covert or overt argument.

RULE 8

The only person you can control is yourself. You can't change others. Stop interpreting disagreements as personal attacks. Remember, he probably feels the same way about you.

RULE 9

Declare "I am responsible. I am cause in the matter." Examine your thinking, your motives. The dislike you feel can be rooted in envy or fearful reminders of dreaded past events. All the blame and fault, all the justification allows you to not be responsible for the health of the partnership. If you succumb to the thinking, "It's all his fault, isn't it?" and "Here's why it is his fault!" the partnership is doomed.

RULE 10

The costs are high to unravel established partnerships -- and the benefits are not nearly as high. It will cost you lots of money, well being, staff performance, patients and peace of mind. What are benefits? The principal benefit is you get to be *right*. You and you alone must decide – would you rather be right or be happy?

THE BERMUDA TRIANGLE
Solo to Associate to Partner

I took in an associate a little over 16 months ago after 18 years in general practice. My revenues had reached $1.16 million. The staff was performing well and was pretty stable. I was overwhelmed with more work than I could handle.

I had been following the advice of consultants who counseled me to increase my revenues and numbers of new patients by adding three more days of production a month so I could better accommodate a new associate when he came on board.

The way the associate-partnership deal was structured was after two years the associate would begin to purchase 50% of the practice over a five-year period. I found a really good kid, local boy with lots of community ties. He had done well in dental school, taken a general dental residency and was married with one young child -- and we even attended the same church. My wife and staff really liked him and it felt like a really good fit.

The first six months together were gangbusters. Production, new patients and hygiene were at all-time highs. But here we are, a year and half later, and everything has slowed way down and I'm having trouble filling the book.

I am not sure this whole thing is going to work out. I'm considering letting him go. I feel terrible. Did I do something wrong?

o   o   o

Your slowdown is nearly universal among dentists in the associate-to-partner process. It is not uncommon after the initial excess business is used up that there is a significant deceleration. In fact, I tell my clients to expect it. I also coach my clients to pre-empt it.

If you are like most dentists, as the practice languishes in this slowdown phase, tension grows in the relationship between you and your associate-dentist. The interactions become strained. Overhead is most likely up and the future looks ominous. Stress is way up because business is way down.

When your associate first came on board, there was a hefty backlog of business – the schedule was full for six to eight weeks, there were numbers of patients waiting to be seen, lots of treatment yet to be provided and cases piling up in the lab waiting to be delivered. Furthermore, recall patients were waiting to be scheduled because, with all the new patients, hygiene appointments were not as available. But isn't that why you got an associate?

The fact is you have now used up your surplus. You've lost your momentum. Now what? Well, it is a matter of generating new business. But you aren't prepared. You haven't been in action nor managing yourself and your associate to generate new business, have you?

More than likely, as things have spiraled down, you pushed whatever new patients and production over to your side of the schedule – which leaves your associate with less to do. He isn't in action to create new patients for himself. He is not generating new treatment to deliver. He is not generating production. But why should he? He didn't have to before and doesn't have the wherewithal at this time to create these outcomes.

Worse, the staff, seeing you stressed-out, blames the associate for the problem. So the staff is now making the associate wrong and blaming him for the current problems in the practice. In fact, so are you. And the associate feels it. Most likely your associate feels guilty and ashamed. The lack of results, the lack of productivity and the altered relationship with you and the staff now has the associate feeling totally isolated, markedly less valued and a burden. The cycle is well on its way to his exit.

I know that some transition consultants say build your practice up so the associate has a practice while you cut back to a more normal schedule. But even in these cases, it is not uncommon after the additional surplus of patients and production is used up that the associate just doesn't have the skill set to keep it going.

Classic mistake. A mistake made over and over again in dental practices involved in the associate-to-partnership process. It would have been a lot more effective to educate, train and manage your associate to market right from the start. While handling some of the surplus, the associate could have also been gearing up his capacity to generate new patients, to deliver treatment plans and to learn how to gain case acceptance. But your associate was nourished on handling surplus, not creating new business.

In my work with clients and their new associates, I strongly recommend that the senior dentist and the associate set clear and specific action plans and goals for the associate for marketing and generating new patients right from the beginning. We ask the senior dentist to be accountable to train and develop the associate in case presentation and closing the deal. It has been our experience that the sooner the associate can generate new patients and production on his or her own, the better the entire process will work. And, yes, the poor senior dentist has to continue to work his butt off and deal with the surplus. But over one to two year's time, the surplus can be ratcheted down to a decent level.

In order to turn your current situation around, you will first need to be responsible. You did a lousy job setting your associate up to win. You didn't work with him from the beginning to enable him to market and to generate new patients. You didn't assist and coach him to do solid exams and treatment plans. You didn't mentor him on how to deliver successful case presentations. No, you used him like an auxiliary dentist to clean up the work you couldn't get to hoping business would continue to expand.

And as we know, hope is a terrible action plan.

It's time to go back and work with your associate on fundamentals. Time to set goals, targets and actions plans for your associate. Time for you to be a real partner and mentor. The way he needs to learn the ropes is for you to show him the ropes.

MOVING FROM OLDER TO ELDER

I just turned 66 this year. I sold my practice three years ago and became an associate a year ago. I can tell my younger partner wants me out. He wants to be in charge. He wants to lead. He wants to make changes. He wants to make more money. But somehow with me there he feels he can't. I am feeling like an "old fart" getting in the way.

I have been practicing dentistry for nearly 40 years. I can't see retiring – I still have my health and love working. But to tell you the truth, I am also scared of getting old.

I know my partner is growing more and more intolerant and I can feel the pressure mounting to get me out.

What should I do?

o   o   o

I understand. Your problem is universal. I have done a lot of work in the aging process as well as with dentists in your situation. I very much appreciate your feelings and your situation.

If you're like most dentists in your situation, looking at yourself in the mirror in unguarded moments, you realize you are growing old. Feelings of loneliness and vulnerability descend. Fears of becoming a geriatric case bubble up. You envision yourself following the predictable pattern – retirement, painful physical decline, a rocking chair existence in a nursing home and the eventual dark and inevitable end to your life.

You react. You throw yourself headlong into your practice and your private life. You must make yourself completely occupied, fully scheduled, your presence absolutely required, with no time for yourself. Yet beneath the surface, when you are by yourself and all alone, something still stirs in your depths about aging that leaves you anxious.

No matter how hectic you make your life, you just can't shake the feeling that old age means wrinkled skin and chronic disease. But how can this be avoided when you are constantly pressed flat against our youth-oriented culture with their aerobically perfect bodies – forcing you to focus obsessively on the physical diminishments that come with aging?

According to traditional models of dental practice, you have already ascended the ladder of your career; you have reached and passed the zenith of your success and influence in the latter part of midlife. Your undeclared, yet clear, realization is this is giving way to a slow and inevitable decline that will eventually culminate in weak, unproductive old age.

I believe there is a totally different and empowering context to create for yourself. In fact, I deliver a program for dentists in their mid-60s and beyond to generate this context and to help them "unlearn" what they have learned about aging.

Rather than simply becoming older, strive to become an elder. By becoming an elder, you create a totally new context and approach to aging. By becoming an elder, you eliminate the deep-seated fear and loathing of growing old. Becoming an elder opens up totally new possibilities of aging where wisdom, serenity, balance, self-knowledge – that represents the fruit of life experience – are held as rewards of aging. By embracing these rewards, the ability to access the world of timelessness, spirit and eternal truths becomes readily available to you.

By becoming an elder you can create your next stage of life and discover what you should be doing for the last quarter of your life. In this context, leaving the practice is something you will want to do, not something you are forced to do. Why? Because you have something that is powerfully calling you into the future.

You can't avoid getting older, stop it or slow it down.

You can't alter the eventual outcome.

You can, however, change the way you think, behave and feel about yourself in the latter part of your life. And if you can do that, you can have a life and future work go far beyond dental practice. A life and a body of work that is fully satisfying, challenging and rewarding.

"A man is not old until regrets take the place of dreams."
~ John Barrymore

"How old would you be if you didn't know how old you were?"
~ Satchel Paige

CORE VALUES: TRUE OR FALSE

You often talk about core values. I am taking on a new associate and I recall that you recommend that senior dentists and incoming dentists agree on core values. I think I know what my core values are, but how can I really be certain?

o   o   o

I work with lots of associateships and partnerships and my starting point is always core values. Why? Because when the core values are not aligned or the core values are violated, the relationship always breaks down. Always! No amount of accommodation by either party will eliminate the damage done when a core value is dishonored. Once this occurs, the relationship begins to unravel and is very difficult to restore.

But your question is: How do I know my core values are "real" core values? Here's my formula for assuring your core values are really core values.

Core Values = Commitments = Money + Time + Energy

To make sure you have accurately defined your core values, write down those values you unconditionally honor, those things you hold sacrosanct – integrity, quality, excellence, fairness, whatever.

Now step back and take stock of your day-to-day actions. You might notice a gap between the things you say you really value and the way you actually spend your time, money and energy. Any gap raises questions about the authenticity of your core values.

Core values ought to be overriding guides to commitments you make every day in the practice. Commitments generate actions taken in the present that bind you and your practice to a future.

Now I am not talking about those huge commitments like Oracle's acquisition of PeopleSoft or Boeing betting the entire company on the 777. In dentistry, it might be you closing down a third of your practice one day, totally disengaging from all your PPO relations with your insurance companies, going strictly fee-for-service.

No, I am talking about those commitments that are even more binding than the "meta" commitments described above. I am talking about those commitments that are so mundane as to be almost invisible. For example, you purchase a particular kind of implant and really like it. Over time it becomes your implant system of choice. You feel comfortable with these fixtures. You are using them nearly all the time. Results are pretty good. Soon the implant company seduces you into being a spokesperson, which further locks you into this implant system. Although you might claim one of your core values is "excellence," because you are now locked into using only one kind of implant, you won't use another type to see if you can produce an even better result with your patients. Those unexamined commitments you made along the way don't support your declared core value. In fact, they demonstrate just the opposite.

Or you might be a seasoned specialist who concentrates his marketing efforts on his key referrals – those referrals that send you lots of cases. However, one of those key referrals does less-than-ethical dentistry, but because he supplies you with a very high number of new patients, you continue to market to him. Although you declare one of your core values as "optimum dental care," your time, your actions and your energy don't reflect this core value.

Another example is you might claim the "Golden Rule" as a core value. "Do unto others ... treat staff like we would like to be treated ourselves ... etc." Nevertheless, you gossip about your hygienist with your office manager. You're not walking the walk.

So, I'm asking you to do some reverse engineering. Keep the core values you wrote down in front of you. Now honestly look at where you spend your energy, time and money. This will reveal your commitments. Since commitments are a direct expression of your true core values, stand in your commitments and be honest about what are your true core values.

Energy + Money + Time = Commitments = Core Values

There are some good books to assist you in distinguishing core values:

The Soul of Business by Tom Chappell

Built to Last by Collins and Porras

Beyond Entrepreneurship by Collins

The 8th Habit by Covey

When your energy, time and money, your commitments and your core values all line up, that's when your core values are truly operational. That's when you have integrity with your core values. When your core values, your commitments and your time, money and energy all are aligned, you will be empowered. When the integrity is out, when these elements are not aligned, then you will be disempowered, because you will be hypocritical.

Some dentists declare core values that they think they should have, such as quality, excellence, fairness. By doing the exercise described above, you will reveal whether your declared core values are truthful or phony. If accurate, great. If phony, dump them. Or if you feel they truly are your core values and you have been violating them – clean up your act.

IT'S NOT YOUR FAULT

I have just been given notice. I have been an associate for a well-established orthodontic practice for 18 months, setting up a whole new life with my wife and baby in a new town and buying a house. After all that hard work, I failed. I've never failed in my career before. I'm really depressed. What am I going to do?

The senior partner has been there more than 20 years. When I began, the practice had two locations and looked like it could have easily expanded into a third. That's one reason he brought on an associate. New patients and starts were strong. It looked and felt like a sure thing. But toward the end, business slowed down and I was viewed as the problem.

I was an outstanding student. I know my stuff. I am a very hard worker. I'm a good guy. But I never quite got my feet on the ground.

For the last four months, Michael always seemed upset with me. He kept chastising me for not generating enough of my own referrals and new patients. But that wasn't easy because, one, I had no idea how to do it and, two, he had burned some bridges with referring docs and, for the most part, had most of the dentists referring to him already.

Recently, he really jumped on my case for not participating more in our staff meetings, not standing up more, not making more demands of staff, not being more of leader. My problem was I wasn't sure what to do, when to be a leader or a manager or even how to be a leader. I didn't want to step on his toes.

I really wanted to become a partner in this practice. Everything seemed to go wrong. What should I have done?

o   o   o

I deeply appreciate your situation. What happened to you is fairly common in the dental industry. In fact, I'd say it is more common that associateships don't work out. It's not personal and has much less to do with you than you think.

Although it's not well documented, when you analyze the ADA's survey data over the last decade, it appears that the failure rate of associates is quite high. Why do so many associateships fail? It's simple. Most associateships are simply designed to fail.

I know you think you did something wrong, that you blame yourself, feel guilty and are suffering. But more than likely the way the entire associateship was set up and structured, anyone in your shoes would have been unsuccessful.

If I took you and put you in a situation where you had to start your own practice, you would, first of all, take an entirely different set of actions than you did in your former practice. You would be more decisive. You would be much more market-driven. You would be more bold and direct with staff. In essence, you would be a much more effective and courageous leader and manager.

What diminished your sense of power and weakened your actions as a leader and manager when you joined the orthodontic practice as an associate? Why did you shrink in bravery and why were your actions not very effective? I assert the reason associates don't come up to speed quickly is the existing context of the practices they join. And as I always say, context is decisive.

The original owner began with a context based on entrepreneurial spirit. He had his survival right in his face. He had to produce. He had to market. He had to hire and fire. If he didn't, he was done for. He was thrown into a live-or-die situation right from the beginning. None of those elements were available to you in the context of the practice when you joined it.

That context possessed a lot of what I call "at stake-ness." He began his practice with very high risk and was fully at stake to make the practice work. No back door. No net. Jump!

But that context morphed into one that contained much less risk, much less "at stake-ness." The context was more about stability, increased effectiveness and greater efficiency. Within three years of opening the doors, how the practice performed, how it did its thing was solidly fashioned.

The upside is that this evolved context worked to produce a highly successful orthodontic practice. The downside is it no longer possessed conditions that could successfully empower a new provider.

Now, as an associate, you step into that existing, evolved context. The outcome for you as an associate was inevitable. Doom.

Unlike other businesses in other industries, dentists don't begin their practices with the intent to have multiple practitioners. No, they build practices to give themselves great jobs and make lots of money. But after years of operation and certain levels of performance, the thought finally occurs: "I need a partner." And by that time, the context, the culture, the condition, the "way it is around here" is fully formed.

So a new associate tries to discern how to act and succeed in that already-established context. The senior partner forgets it was the tension of "Are we going to make it?" that propelled him to take risks, be courageous, stand up as a leader. Although he says he wants the associate to take risks, at the same time, he really doesn't because it might disrupt what he already has.

Like many associates, you didn't have a context that supported risk-taking, a context that directly put you at stake. Rather, you had a context that suppressed your need to lead, manage and market.

But the senior dentist wanted you to perform as he did in the beginning. To take risks. To market. To work tirelessly. How can you act that way when the context doesn't support that thinking and those actions? Bottom line, you can't. It was a no-win situation.

So, your situation wasn't set up for you to win. I'd love to get hold of dentists who are going the associate-partner route and coach them to develop the context and content of their practices so that associates and future partners can win. But that would mean they'd have to know that what they have now is insufficient, that it isn't going to work to generate a successful associate. It's hard to tell successful dentists what to do. Success many times breeds arrogance. Maybe by the third associate, your former boss will get the message.

SHE DOESN'T ACT LIKE AN OWNER

I have had an associate for three years in my 17-year-old practice. She is now interested in buying in as a partner, a prospect we set up for her in the beginning with our agreement. But she has really shown little interest in managing or leading the staff. I have had her pay the bills on occasion to get a better idea of our overhead, but she just doesn't seem to have the drive to consider cost control.

I realize that I am not comfortable sharing decisions with her because she just doesn't want to put in the time to really be an owner. She wants to buy equity, but doesn't seem to understand any of the risks or responsibilities of ownership. I have tried to teach her by example, but don't feel that I'm getting through. Am I too controlling? Or is my intuition correct, that she isn't cut out for partnership?

○   ○   ○

You are not too controlling. You are being an owner – a good owner, one who isn't going to complete an offer for equity purchase unless the associate clearly demonstrates he or she can deliver and perform.

Your problem is common to many. Your issue, if unaddressed, is what begins the demise of the relationship. Although the contracts, documents and timelines are set, what was not clear from the beginning were the conditions required to be eligible for purchasing an equity share in the practice.

In our work with associateships-to-partnerships, we spend a great deal of time upfront focused on articulating and quantifying the conditions required for equity purchase. We take the assumptions and expectations out, and we introduce clear lines of definition.

That is especially true in the domains of leadership, ownership, management and marketing.

Ordinarily it takes six months for an associate to get up to speed in the delivery of care and patient management. It takes about that long for an associate to move his or her revenues to a place where he or she is paying his or her own salary and contributing to the practice's bottom line.

The senior partner, as you have expressed, has an expectation that the associate will naturally come online as an owner and be responsible, committed, driven and sensitive to generating new patients and revenues. The senior partner has an expectation that the associate will become keenly interested in the expense side of the practice's operations as well.

Expectations unfulfilled lead to upsets. With the associate's apparent lack of interest in and commitment to the business side of the practice, the first crack in the trust, affinity and partnership has already appeared.

Worse, if you're like most dentists, at the seven- to nine-month mark, it is not uncommon for the practice to experience a significant slowdown in new patients and production. All the excess generated when the senior partner was alone is now squeezed out of the practice. During that time, the associate was basically being spoon-fed new patients. The senior partner finds her or his book not quite as full, there are holes in the schedule and the overall production figures are heading in the wrong direction. Now what?

First, I'd take the offer for partnership off the table. Second, I'd sit down with the associate right now and clearly articulate what is expected in his or her behavior and attitude. Address the required intentions in financial management. Set goals in ownership, management, leadership and marketing. Because you missed the train before in speaking with your associate, it will be more difficult now. But you need to sit down and spell it out.

For example, the associate will know in the coming six months that she needs to be marketing and generating eight to 10 new patients of her own each month. She will understand that she needs to be leading and managing particular office projects with key staff members, such as improving recall frequency from 72% to 82%, for example. Do you get the point?

"Win, then play" is our motto. Don't play to win. If you don't clearly and succinctly define the conditions necessary for the associate to become an equity partner in the areas of ownership, leadership, management and marketing, you are hoping it works out – and hope is a terrible business plan.

If you had defined the conditions at the beginning, somewhere between nine months and 12 months later you would have had a very clear picture of whether to complete the offer for equity purchase or take it off the table. My recommendation is that you take the deal off the table for six months and go back and define the conditions.

A FUNCTION OF COMMITMENTS & CONDITIONS

I really like my new associate/soon-to-be partner. In fact, I'd consider her a great friend. I enjoy spending time with her and her family.

My question is this: I tend to avoid conflicts with people I care about and I am sure that partnership will entail conflict. How should I make a plan ahead of time to make sure we get through conflicts with both our friendship and our partnership strong and intact?

o o o

I suggest you put business before friendship. Friendship is support-based. Business is performance-based. If a friend fails, you're there for support. If a partner fails, it hurts your business. Friends avoid conflicts. Business owners literally cause them. Conflicts unbundle situations so they can be reformed into something that performs better. If you can't cause or confront a conflict, you won't be able to address the hard issues or significant breakdowns.

My coaching is to establish conditions of satisfaction before you pull the trigger on partnership. You see, in certain areas of life, like marriage and children, commitments are unconditional. But in business, all commitments are conditional. Operating from commitments makes a partnership work – period. Shared commitments to production, patient care, quality, staff performance and marketing are necessary. If one partner is committed and the other is not, well, you're not going to have partnership very long.

So first, sit down with your future partner and define the commitments that will be needed by both of you to make the practice work – commitments to practice growth, marketing, new patients, case acceptance, increasing revenues, staff performance and so on. Write those commitments down. Convert them into agreements. Send the agreements to your attorney and have him or her craft an addendum from them for signature by both parties – and add it to your Purchase Agreement.

But, as I said above, in business, all commitments are conditional. Now, with the commitments in hand, define the required conditions needed to execute and deliver on them. Conditions can include open and honest communication, straight talk, not withholding, listening to each other and being open to coaching. Come to full alignment on those conditions. Write them down. Now make a commitment to abide by them. Stick to your word about the conditions.

After you define your commitments and conditions, review them on a semi-annual or annual basis, update them and add to them. You will have developed a structure to support you in keeping your partnership strong.

COMMUNICATE EXPECTATIONS & CONCERNS OR...

I am the senior dentist in my 15-year-old practice, with a partner of two years. Mostly, my partner and I get along well, with similar clinical styles and a commitment to good customer service. Because almost everything is going well, I have been overlooking some things that really bug me about my partner. He is brusque and even rude to some of our staff when he is in a hurry or behind schedule. And he rarely stays to make sure the office is secure in the evenings, which I always do.

There are a number of other similarly small issues. Sometimes those things are enough to make me long for the old days of being the only boss in the office. Am I just not cut out for partnership or is this guy really a jerk?

○　　○　　○

If you are like most dentists with associates, you don't have sufficient or well-designed meetings with your associate. And when you do, you rarely talk about the issues that cause a partnership to fail. Relationship issues. Communication issues. Behavioral issues. Attitudes. Values. Nope, those are the things you avoid talking about and hope they somehow miraculously get better. Let me say once again that "hope" never produces a result.

With my clients, I strongly recommend establishing structured and consistent partnership meetings. I ask them to begin each meeting by asking two questions.

1. What expectations do you have of me that you are not telling me?

2. What concerns, if any, have come up for you about me – my performance or behavior – that are bothering you?

Expectations unfulfilled lead to upsets, and upsets invariably cause division, distancing and emotional turmoil. A senior partner always – and I mean always – has expectations of how an associate should behave and perform. And those expectations continue to expand as the associate achieves different levels of performance. For example, after an associate achieves a particular level of revenue performance, there arises an expectation in marketing, managing staff and improving diagnosis and treatment planning. When those expectations are met, there are other expectations that arise in terms of ownership, management and professional participation.

From the associate's side, there are expectations about how you, the senior partner, will act. Introducing him to patients. Giving him new patients. Teaching him how to interact with patients and do case presentations. Coaching him on how to manage staff. Educating him on how the money works.

The point is there will always be expectations by both parties of each other – always. And if those expectations are not communicated, they will invariably lead to upsets. Asking the question "What expectations do you have of me that you are not telling me?" will require each partner to state those things that eventually could undermine and unravel the partnership.

As a senior partner, you hold the practice as your baby. The same way you cautiously observe someone interacting with your toddler and view or interpret some of his or her actions as inappropriate or indifferent, you observe your associate as he interfaces with the various parts of the practice. Does he treat the staff with respect? Does he hold patients as a sacred resource? Is he too flippant with parents? Does he honor what you've built? Like expectations, concerns will continuously arise.

Concerns not communicated build in mass and depth. Concerns not communicated become truths. Concerns not communicated become reality. So by asking "What concerns, if any, have come up for you about me – my performance or behavior – that are bothering you?" you pre-empt the aftermath of uncommunicated concerns, which can be devastating.

I strongly recommend no less than one partnership meeting every month – and that you hold it as a top priority. And at that meeting, begin by asking those two questions. Do that and you will pre-empt many issues that arise in your partnership. You can easily handle him being brusque and rude inside either of these two questions.

THE ASSOCIATE'S JOURNEY

I have been an associate in a general practice for the last nine months. I came out of a general practice residency. The associateship was to lead to partnership.

When I began, the relationship with "Bill" was full of high energy, camaraderie, support, sharing and collegiality. But now I feel lots of tension and even some resentment.

Over the last nine months, I have brought my clinical skills quickly up to par. I've increased my patient communication skills and case presentation skills and I can get most patients to accept my treatment recommendations. My revenues have been increasing each month. I'm now doing around $27,000 a month.

Bill and I did everything by the book: a Letter of Intent, mutually approved appraisal value, a very fair Associate/Employment Agreement and, although not yet signed, a mutually approved Purchase Agreement. But last week, when I asked about completing the purchase agreement, he said he wasn't sure I was ready and he stated that he might want to wait.

Wait for what?

When I ask him if there's anything wrong, he says there isn't. When I ask him if there is anything I am doing wrong, he says, "Not really."

I am beginning to get cold feet for this deal.

Your advice?

o   o   o

What you are going through is commonplace in the associate-to-partner process. Your senior partner is upset, although he doesn't even realize it. What is causing that upset is he has certain expectations of your performance in areas beyond clinical delivery and patient management that are not being fulfilled. Unfulfilled expectations always lead to upsets.

There are a number of stages to master for an associate to reach partner. The first three should be accomplished in the first year or so. Until each stage is accomplished, we recommend an associate not be permitted to move forward toward becoming a co-owner.

The three stages in the first 12 months are:

Stage 1 - Clinical Competency

Stage 2 - Effective Patient Management

Stage 3 - Ownership/Effective Marketing

The associate has to successfully pass these four stages in the second year:

Stage 4 - Ownership/Money, Finances and Economic Drivers

Stage 5 - Leadership

Stage 6 - Manager

Stage 7 - Partner and Co-Owner

One stage remains in the third year:

Stage 8 - Director of the Board

Each stage has its own rites of passage. Because you're in the first year of your associateship, we'll specifically address these three stages.

Stage 1 and Stage 2 are basically an extension of an associate's training and education in dental school, residency or graduate training. The third stage, however, is unlike anything an associate has ever encountered before. It exists within a different context.

Succeeding in Stage 3 requires different skill sets, different thinking and different commitments than are ordinarily present in an associate.

Stage 3 is one of the toughest stages to accomplish. In fact, most associateships fall apart because Stage 3 is not successfully achieved. And, like your situation, that ordinarily occurs toward the end of the first year or beginning of the second year of the associateship.

Achieving clinical competency is learning to provide dental care within the practice's established standards of time and quality and its systems – "The way we do it in this practice." That is the easiest stage to master. Most dentists are primed and ready to achieve the necessary skill sets and knowledge to deliver quality care in a timely fashion, in line with how it is done in the practice.

Effective patient management is the next stage. Here an associate learns to interact with patients in such a way that patients accept the associate as a "real" dentist and will follow his or her requests and directives. Again, it's a stage in which most associates achieve success in a fairly short period of time. Associates generally have enough background in patient management, anchored to a true commitment to taking care of patients, that this stage is soon accomplished.

But it's after Stage 2 when things usually get stalled or begin to unravel.

The "Effective Marketing" piece of the ownership puzzle is the stage where an associate is suddenly confronted. The senior partner has an expectation that the associate will now act like an owner. And a critical accountability of ownership is generating new patients.

In Stage 3, the associate becomes answerable to the practice to produce new patients. This is when the associate must face up to an implicit requirement that he or she needs to directly contribute to the bottom line. Until then, it wasn't even in his or her consciousness.

Now he or she needs to interact with patients and the community in such a way that new patients are referred to the practice.

It's a stage that neither the associate nor the senior partner generally anticipates. The senior partner has been an owner for a long time. He or she never thought the primary job as an owner was to generate new patients. He or she has been doing it ever since starting the practice and now it's second nature.

On the other hand, for the first seven to nine months, the associate is working on existing patients or patients referred to the practice. The associate is basically unaware of the work and interactions required to generate new patients.

But by seven to nine months into the associateship, the excess patients are all used up. Restorative dentistry from the recalls has been picked clean. The senior dentist has taken all his or her vacations. But now, back at work, the senior dentist is experiencing some holes or lightness in his or her schedule. He or she wants to get busy again. The senior dentist stops transferring patients that could be on his or her schedule to the associate. The senior dentist wants to get production back on track.

Suddenly, the senior dentist realizes that to increase revenues, where this whole deal makes sense, the associate needs to generate new business. Unfortunately, like you, most associates don't have a clue how to do that.

The senior dentist had an expectation that the associate would operate and perform like him or her. The senior dentist expected the associate would naturally generate new patients from existing patients and that the associate would go out into the community and generates business. Well, expectations unfulfilled lead to upsets. And that's my guess as to the problem: Your senior partner is upset.

Marketing has a long gestation period. It takes time to market and have it begin to produce results. In our work, we strongly recommend that an associate start marketing right from the get-go, not seven months later. We spend time with the senior partner and associate to generate an associate marketing plan with a task list and timelines. We coach the senior partner and associate to target referred new patients from the associate right from the beginning.

I suggest you sit down with your senior partner and do something you should have done when you began - delineate your practice's conditions of satisfaction. Conditions of satisfaction are those conditions required for an associate to join a practice and to become an equal partner.

Then define a) **WHO** you need to be in the practice, b) **HOW** you need to behave, c) **WHAT** you need to accomplish and by when, d) what **COMMITMENTS** are required, e) how you need to **RELATE** to staff and patients and f) what **RESULTS** you need to produce and by when those results should be produced. Be as specific as possible. Most likely none of these conditions are detailed in your current documents and agreements, yet they are the source of most associate-to-partnerships failures.

Here's an example of a condition of satisfaction: By the last quarter of your first year, you will be able to market to existing patients and people in the community so that a minimum of eight new patients a month are generated from your marketing efforts.

Then, working with some transition advisers, we transform the conditions of satisfaction into agreements. The agreements are formed into an addendum and made part of both the Associate Agreement and the Purchase Agreement.

In our consulting, work we employ this eight-stage model. But understand it's our own model. We invented it; it is not the "truth." It's what works in our hands, with our clients. I am sure other consulting entities have their own models and they work equally well in their hands.

The Conditions of Satisfaction → Agreements → Addendum process is another one of our inventions. Our experience is it works, keeps people out of trouble and, most important, has them clarify those areas that cause breakdowns. Some transition companies welcome this input. They embrace collaboration. A few other transition companies prefer not to work in a collaborative fashion and so we have to work around them and not with them.

DON'T WIMP OUT ON DIFFICULT CONVERSATIONS

I have an associate of one year who will be buying in as a partner next year. I really like him, and we seem to have the potential for a great partnership. The problem is I really don't like his wife. She comes in the office and offers her opinions about things to our staff as if she were the partner. My spouse has never been involved in the office, and I like it that way. I'm not sure how to handle the situation. Please help.

○   ○   ○

You've got a real and partnership-threatening problem. You need to take the risk and confront it. It might cause your relationship to dissolve, but if you don't address it, it will eventually cause it to dissolve anyway. So I strongly suggest you address it, the sooner the better.

But how do you address such a personal and threatening issue? How do you bring up something that will undoubtedly cause a huge breakdown? First, you must realize there are two parts to handling this kind of problems. It's not that it will be hard to bring up the issue. What's stopping you is your fear of the aftermath. You're scared because you don't know how he'll respond. You're scared it will throw the whole thing out of kilter. You're scared it will create an irresolvable problem. If you let fear stop you, you will regret it until it becomes so unbearable that you break up the partnership.

So begin by confessing your feelings and your fears. "John, I need to talk to about something that I fear will cause a major problem in our relationship. It might cause us to break up our partnership. And I have no idea how to handle the situation."

Next, **tell him what you are afraid he will think, do or say once you address the issue.** "John, I'm not sure how you'll respond once I tell you about this issue. You might get mad, upset, withdrawn – but I know if I don't address this issue, it's going to cause major problems."

Finally, **say it as if you might be wrong**. "John, my issue is I am having real difficulty with your wife. She comes in the office and offers her opinions about things to our staff as if she were a partner. My spouse has never been involved in the office, and I like it that way for us both. I'm not sure how to handle the situation. What do you suggest?"

Follow those three steps. They are a tactic for handling conflicts that works. Besides, if you don't address it, it's going to eat you up and undermine your partnership until it causes it to break up.

WIN, THEN PLAY
Committing to Each Other's Success

I've had two associates who didn't work out. They both began the same way, with high hopes and great expectations, but then over time fell apart. Things start to break down until I can't put up with the associate and I have to let him or her go.

It's beginning again. My current associate doesn't see emergency care like I do. I see emergency care as an important area of marketing and customer service, and I come in at all hours to handle emergencies as well as quickly address any patient concerns. My new associate/partner feels that most things can wait until Monday and just handles things over the phone. So far, I haven't addressed that with him, but it is getting to be a problem on Monday mornings now.

I'd like him to work out, but it feels like I'm going down the same tunnel all over again. What should I do?

o   o   o

Issues and differences are inherent in any partnership. If you have an associate, if you have a partnership, you will always have differences. The question becomes: "What do you need to resolve differences effectively?"

Two people will always see the world differently. It is not uncommon for an associate/partner to see differences in many areas of practice – clinical delivery, financial management, staff performance or, in your case, emergency care protocol. Nothing in the practice is immune from an associate/partner seeing things differently.

You'd better come to grips with the fact that if you have a partnership, you will always have differences. So how do you resolve those differences? Do you compromise? Succumb? Surrender? Dominate? Command? Try to get consensus? Give up? Do it yourself and stew about it?

In our work, we educate, train and develop partners to make their decisions based on policy. Policy provides an overriding approach of processing how partners decide. But even with policy, another fundamental and critical element needs to be in place, one that is so elemental it is often overlooked. That is an authentic commitment to each other's success. Without that, no matter what you do, the partnership will fail.

Often, for example, the senior dentist hesitates to commit to the associate's success *until* he or she demonstrates he or she can produce, *until* he or she demonstrates he or she is clinically able, *until* he or she can manage staff, *until* he or she introduces new patients – the "untils" can go on forever.

That waiting to commit creates a barrier, a kind of filter through which the other's actions are interpreted. "If he or she did this, then I'd be committed." Without a commitment to each other's success, there is inherently a lack of trust, a lack of affinity and a lack of kinship. How can you resolve differences without trust, affinity and kinship? The answer is: "You can't."

Without a commitment to each other's success, you judge, assess, interpret and perceive the other cautiously, guardedly, often questioning his or her intent.

Performance and results are always enhanced when backed by another's commitment to your success. Performance and results are always diminished when another doubts you, judges you, assesses you, questions you – trying to evaluate your worthiness before committing.

Now, I am not saying you shouldn't be tough and rigorous with each other. But when a coach and a player are committed to each other's success, they can be twice as hard on each other – because they trust each other.

My motto is "Win, then play." Without a commitment to the other's success, you are playing to win. With a commitment to each other's success, you are winning, then playing.

If you can't commit to each other's success from the beginning, don't do the deal. And, yes, I understand that when you commit, you risk getting burned. And, yes, I understand that all commitments are conditional. But if you don't take the risk and are unable to make the commitment to each other's success, the partnership has little chance of succeeding.

THE ONE THING

I am about to go down the path of associate-to-partner. I have been in practice 22 years, have a very profitable practice, a good staff and more new patients than I can handle.

I have heard all the horror stories from my colleagues. I have been to two presentations touting the incredible success of associate-to-partner ventures. Seems like reality lies somewhere in between.

What prompted me to write to you is I just finished watching "City Slickers" with Billy Crystal. Curly, Jack Palance, kept on talking about "the one thing." What would you say is "the one thing" to make a partnership work?

o   o   o

As you realize, the associate-to-partner path is complex. You have numerous factors at play in the process – personal income, financial positioning, tax consequences, practice performance, provider performance, staff behavior and personality, marketing, new patients, different psychologies, different personalities, different backgrounds of experience, different ages and cultural and generational differences. Not to mention local, regional, national and even international elements. But when I ponder the question "What's the one thing?" the answer is always the same. The "one thing" is a shared future.

If each partner envisions a different future, the partnership doesn't have a chance. That doesn't mean the senior partner doesn't have as part of his or her future slowing down, cutting down to two days a week and eventually retiring. Nor does it mean the junior partner doesn't envision building a larger office with all kinds of computer gear and the latest technologies. But what absolutely must be present is a mutually shared future that both can clearly see and articulate – a future big enough to hold both of their individual futures.

Why is a mutual, shared future so fundamental and critical? The reason is that future has a very unique quality. A future possesses "possibility," and nowhere else will you find possibility. You won't find possibility in the past. You won't find possibility in the present. You will only find possibility in the future. (Please read *The Art of Possibility* by Zander)

You won't find possibility in explanation, narrative, judgment, assessment, evaluation, complaint or opinion. These are past tense and the past has no possibility. The past is already decided. It's done. Over. Finished. Complete!

Only in a future will you find possibility – and possibility has a profound impact on a relationship, especially a partner relationship. When something is possible, you see the future as able to be achieved. And, as important, you see yourself as able and effective in accomplishing it. Possibility is a context of "it shall be."

When leaders speak, they speak of a compelling future – a vision – so that others see and believe it is possible. Once people see it as possible, they are willing to commit to making it happen. So possibility can engender commitment. And in a partnership, what cements the union is common commitment – a shared commitment to a future.

When two lovers engage in a shared future, they bring about possibility. What happens when possibility is present? Their relationship becomes much closer and the differences become much less important. So possibility engenders kinship, empathy, trust and appreciation.

When two friends decide to go on a canoeing trip together, there is a shared future that is full of possibility. So possibility engenders camaraderie, friendship and affinity.

What kind of future are we talking about here? We're talking about a future that both partners can see and speak. A future that isn't about the past – but that stands on the past. A future that is not about each individual partner, but includes each individual partner. A future that makes a difference for the practice and patients. A future that both partners hold as possible.

I recommend you sit down with your future partner and go through the process of articulating a future for the practice. A future that will hold your "exiting" future. A future that will hold his or her long-term and immediate future. A future that both of you see and feel is truly possible.

We use a particular model for developing practice and partnership futures based on the work of Jim Collins described in his books *Good to Great* and *Beyond Entrepreneurship*. But there are lots of very solid models out there that work and good consultants who can assist you in this process.

PARTNERSHIP PITFALLS

I am working with a transition consultant and have just begun the process of finding my future partner. I see you always give straight, no-nonsense advice.

The consultant doing the transition knows his stuff, but I have a feeling he doesn't understand the underlying dynamics of having a successful partnership. What is your advice on having a successful partnership that lasts?

○   ○   ○

Many great partnerships have gone the way of Martin and Lewis, Gilbert and Sullivan, Shaq and Kobe and Caesar and Brutus. No matter how close the friendship, there's always the chance one or the other will take a knife in the back – or, like Caesar, in the front. So how do you create a partnership that endures?

Most dentists think the answer is compromise. And they would be dead wrong. Never compromise. Never!

The first rule of great partnerships that last is there is "no holding back" when it comes to what's happening in the practice. When one brings up an idea, the other ought to try to shoot it down. You need to find something you both like or don't do it. Don't compromise.

This setup might seem too "charged" for many dentists, since they are usually risk-averse and avoid conflict at all costs. But honest collaboration is a cornerstone for a successful partnership. Collaboration has nothing to do with being pals.

Partnerships that are about "having a great friend" are doomed to failure. Being a great partner has nothing to do with being a great friend. Friends usually believe they know each other well, so they stop pressing and doing due diligence because they "already know" the other person and what he or she will think, do or say. They don't want to damage the friendship, so they compromise.

I recommend partners maintain a significant barrier between work and play. Keep the partnership focused on improving the practice. The partnership relationships should be in service to the business, not maintaining peace and harmony in the relationship.

Being a good partner has nothing to do with being a good friend!

It is not uncommon that within a reasonable period of time, the practice starts doing well. That is the time the partnership stops doing well. You see, once the business survival is handled, what comes to the foreground are values. If core values are not authentically shared, aren't held with equal passion and reverence, then the partners start to question each other, distrust each other and avoid each other. Core values are the underpinning of all business decisions and when the values are not shared, the partnership starts to unravel.

In our work with partnerships, we use a number of processes to make sure the values are clarified between partners. In fact, we use a "governance structure" to ensure these values are primary drivers in business, personnel and partnership decisions.

We use several personality tests – the Enneagram and the Now, Discover Your Strengths, for example – to discover where there will be synergy and where there will be disconnects. We have a defined structure for partnership meetings so areas of contention are directly addressed. And, we generate partnership guidelines by presenting hypothetical situations to the partnership like:

What if you bring on another partner?

What if one of you gets divorced?

What if a key employee gets caught stealing?

What if one of the partners wants out early?

Lastly, and what I find most important in having successful partnerships, is keep your word with your partner and your business. Integrity – honoring yourself as your word – in and for the partnership is fundamental, critical and essential. Don't do this and you might as well throw in the towel for the partnership.

HOW TO DECIDE HOW TO DECIDE

I am an associate about to sign final papers to purchase 50% of a large general practice. We used a national consulting company for the transition. It's going to cost me about $5,000 a month for five years plus a balloon payment at the end. My future partner expects to practice another 10 years. Things so far have gone pretty well, but some real concerns are beginning to surface.

In the two years I have been an associate, my production has grown to approximately $57K a month. I feel comfortable with the staff and patients. I feel good about my abilities in diagnosis, treatment planning and delivery. I am now participating with the Panky Institute, so I am learning a tremendous amount and I have a lot of enthusiasm for delivering very high-quality care.

But I can see that in a year or two I will want to make some changes in the practice and I have a feeling this will cause problems. I want to go in some new directions clinically (implants, high-end restorative and cosmetic care). I want to be totally digital, lots of imaging, computers in each operatory, etc. And I'd like a more robust Web presence for marketing. I also want to make some much-needed staff changes of some very long-term employees.

Every time I bring these subjects up, my future partner seems unconcerned and seems not to take me very seriously. What I hear is: "It's working just fine. Why change? I've been doing this for 25 years. The staff knows their jobs. You'll learn."

I'd like this partnership to work, but my suspicions are he's going to do only what he wants to do and discount what I want to do.

Your advice? Is this just a case of pre-partnership jitters?

○　○　○

What you are experiencing is not uncommon. In fact, it is one of the core reasons a majority of dental partnerships fail. In my experience, few transition consultants currently address this part of the partnership equation. Transition consultants know how to set up the deal (appraisals, negotiations, documentation, transactions, financing), but they don't have a proven model for setting up partnerships to work successfully into the future.

My method in partnership development is unique. It builds the partners' skill sets and wherewithal based on a very successful corporate-organizational model. This model is based on our experience of more than 10 years in corporate consulting with the executives and Boards of Directors of several *Fortune* 100 companies (GE Capital, Boeing, Intel) as well as numbers of medium-sized companies ($250 million-plus) such as hospitals and biotech, IT and insurance companies.

Also, having been a member of Techniko, an affiliation of leading-edge corporate consulting firms serving many *Fortune* 1,000 companies, I have learned a bucket-full from my colleagues. And many of the principles that work at the corporate and organizational level can be directly applied to dental partnerships. For example, one principle I learned and have seen work time and time again in successful companies is "policy governs, not people."

I think that most transition consultants insist the partners nail down a practice vision, mission and purpose based on mutually aligned and agreed-upon core values. If your consultant hasn't asked you to do this, my advice is to complete this assignment right away. For me, that is the essential first step. If you can't agree on your core values and vision, the partnership isn't going to work. Period.

Good transition consultants will make you do a budget and business plan with targets for one, three and five years so everyone knows where the enterprise is going and what needs be produced and collected, along with how many new patients are needed to achieve these ends. If this isn't done, you'd better get it done.

Concurrently, in my experience with transition consultants, they guide you through a maze of agreements: Appraisal, Letter of Intent, Associate Agreement and finally the Purchase Agreement and a rewrite of corporate documents. And that's usually as far as it goes. For me, however, that's just the beginning, not the end.

The next step is to convert the partnership from two individuals trying to share running the shop into a professionally managed firm.

Some transition consultants attempt to do this by having the partners define "who will be accountable for what." But in my experience, this accountability structure disintegrates over time. Staff members learn how to manipulate this structure and simply go to the partner who will give them what they want. Disagreements between partners arise and cannot be resolved. Changes occur in technology, delivery of care and staff behavior or performance. And choices about how and where to go in the future are not always easily resolved between the partners. So the performance of the practice suffers, putting more and more stress on the partnership.

So what can be done?

In your corporate documents, you will find two or three pages that describe and define your Board of Directors. Positions, accountabilities, power and, to some extent, the Board's processes and operations. But for most partnerships, this major corporate structure, Board of Directors, is rarely, if ever, utilized. In my work with partners, I develop and use this very powerful vehicle. I educate and train partners to think, act and operate like Board Directors.

The job of the Board is governance. One major piece of governance is generating policy. Remember: *Policy governs, not people.* One policy which I insist be designed near the beginning is a policy that clearly defines how decisions are made. The Board decides how the partnership decides how it decides.

In your case, for example, you'd present a recommendation or a request for a future project or initiative to the Board. It would follow the process of decision-making as defined by policy. So it wouldn't be personal. It wouldn't depend on seniority. It wouldn't be arbitrary or capricious. If the policy is well-written and executed, decisions would have to pass through defined gates and gather the votes before approval. But when ratified, it would be evident that the decision clearly benefited the partners (present and future), the practice and the patients.

Policy is only and always generated from the point of view of what is best for the company, including the present and future owners. Eventually, you and your partner will want to sell your shares. If you develop your Board capacity – the Board's ability to define the ends – to effectively direct senior management and to generate and execute policy, the asset value of the company will increase and the addition of future partners will be much more easily achieved.

The first book to read along this path is *Growing Pains: the Transition from an Entrepreneurship to a Professionally Managed Firm* by Eric Flamholtz.

Having worked with Boards for the last 11 years, in nearly every corporate environment from start-up to mature companies, from small (under $100 million) to large ($11 billion), from very large (260,000 employees) to very small (two-partner dental practices), I am very clear that once a Board becomes fully functional, goes about its business and does its job, the enterprise operates at a much more effective and productive level. With far fewer upsets, problems and issues.

The bottom line: Make sure your partnership is governed by policy and not by people. Then most of the clashing that typically gets in the way of decision-making will disappear and you'll both be much happier in the long run – and you'll absolutely be more successful.

WHAT'S THE FUSS ABOUT GOVERNANCE?

I have two very close colleagues who have a long-term partnership and I have a similar kind of partnership. Our practices are also pretty comparable as well. We have large specialty practices, are considering adding a third partner and have two locations with 12-plus staff. My revenues are slightly less than theirs, at about $2.35 million.

I regard these two individuals as quite smart and successful and, like them, I am always looking to improve my practice. They sing your praises about the work you and Art Haines have done with them on "governance." Both agree that since they developed governance policies for their practice, it has become much easier to run it and there is much less tension and conflict between them.

Please explain to me what they mean by governance and what you worked on with them.

o   o   o

When a practice reaches a particular level of performance, measured in revenues, numbers of staff and patient volume, we suggest owner-dentists consider undergoing an educational, training and development process to operate as a Board of Directors.

Our objective is to develop larger, more successful practices -- particularly if they have multiple owners -- to think, act and execute like a corporation. In our experience, small business models don't work because they base their decisions on an individual dentist's personality and identity. For larger, leading-edge practices, the individual-based, smaller business model doesn't have the capacity to make smart, strategic or even sound operational decisions.

Most practices, by the time they reach leading-edge status, are incorporated, either as an S-Corp, C-Corp, LLC or LLP. Each of these corporate forms is required to have a Board structure according to federal and state mandates. Using this already-defined body to the fullest limit of its corporate license allows the Board of the practice to really govern.

We began this effort because of the significant failure rate in dental partnerships. Having partners operate as a Board removes many of the usual disagreements, upsets and conflicts that occur between partners. But this work quickly unfolded into a legitimate body of knowledge, with an entire set of distinctions and effective processes and outcomes. We are now seeing how well this work can be adapted to many other practice environments.

What does having an effective Board do for a dental practice?

1. It reduces or eliminates conflicts and issues between partners.

2. It establishes formal processes for making critical and fundamental decisions.

3. It enables owners to be more effective, less emotional, more creative and more productive.

4. It directly enhances the operational and negotiable value of the practice.

5. It rapidly enhances the inclusion and integration of future partners into the practice.

6. It significantly increases the capacity of the practice to be effectively transitioned to other dentist-owners.

We are uniquely qualified to deliver this work. We have significant experience in working with corporate Boards, from *Fortune* 500 companies to Silicon Valley startups to large regional medical centers to eight-person physician practices. I don't know of any other practice management consultant who can claim this experience or background of success.

First, we begin our work with dentists to address two fundamental domains:
1) What's the accountability of the Board? and 2) What's the job of the Board?

The first domain soon becomes apparent: The Board of Directors is accountable for the company's resources and capacities being deployed in a way that maximizes the owner's value. Once the dentist-owners understand this accountability, we focus on training and educating them to perform as a Board.

The second domain, the job of the Board, takes time to grasp and to perform. The job of the Board is to govern. Dentists struggle with governance at first, but we have found that every well-functioning Board must in some way answer these four governance questions:

1. What results will the company achieve for the owners (stockholders)?

2. How will we operate as a Board?

3. Who will manage the operations of the company and what results will he/she be responsible for achieving?

4. What authority will be delegated to management?

Now, each practice has its own core values, beliefs, purpose and mission. So we weren't surprised to find that the answers to these governance questions were different and distinct for every practice. One size clearly does not fit all. For our dentist-clients, we begin by restating the governance questions in the following way, then coach them to answer these questions in a way that fits for them:

What are the benefits the practice will generate for the owners?
Current income, deferred income for retirement, increased asset value, professional development and satisfaction, discretionary time.

What are the ground rules we will use for governing the practice?
Decision-making method: consensus, voting, frequency of meetings, agenda setting, participation of new partners in governance.

Who will manage the company and what is that person to accomplish?
Will there be a managing partner and, if so, who will that be; hire/fire decisions for the managing partner office and/or clinical manager; performance objectives; performance evaluations.

What decision-making authority will be delegated to day-to-day management?
Staff hire/fire, performance evaluations, budget management, equipment purchases, spending limits.

In each of these four areas, decisions are written down in the form of policies. Written policies need not be lengthy or cumbersome. The best policies are simple, clear statements.

Written policies support effective operations by providing a way to maintain consistency over time as a practice grows and adds new partners or employed providers. Policies also create a point of reference during times of difficulty or disagreement. Policies allow partners to make a clear statement to prospective new partners about how the practice operates.

By addressing and answering these questions, you can convert these answers into policy. You establish and conduct monthly Board meetings where you perform as Directors of a professional corporation. The Board governs through policy, defines the future by determining the ends and sets expectations for management's performance.

The most rewarding outcome is that governing by policy removes identity, psychology, personality and politics from the practice. And in the end, policy governs, not people.

THE PASSION OF JOHN

I am a 63-year-old general practitioner with a fee-for-service practice that's reasonably successful. The practice grossed a little over $1.27 million in 2004 and is growing slowly. I am looking toward transition, recruiting an associate-to-partner, eventually becoming an associate myself, then exiting at age 67 or so.

I have interviewed several individuals. Two, in particular, demonstrate very sound technical training. They have been associates in other practices, one for three years the other for four. Both are married, have young children. They both want to move to this area and are licensed in the state. Both have attended advanced crown and bridge programs, have studied occlusion and certainly have the ability to carry on the philosophy of excellence of this practice. I am trying to choose between these two dentists. Both are named John.

How do I make my selection between John 1 and John 2? What's the most critical thing I should be looking for?

o   o   o

I remember about 10 years ago, a number of consultant colleagues and I participated in martial arts training. We all commonly used martial arts as a metaphor for our consulting, and yet none of us had any real experience with it.

This adventure began at one of our conferences several months before. After a few beers, a member of our group said, "In martial arts, you use the force of your opponent to win." After a few jokes, and a few more beers, the six of us at the table decided to register for martial arts training. Three months later, we found ourselves at an intensive, two-and-a-half-day program at a training facility in Virginia called Personal Defensive Measures.

It was 5:30 am on a cold and overcast Friday when we first met our instructor, a guy named Thomas McClure. McClure was a tough-looking character in his late 40s, 6 feet tall, weathered face, mean and lean. He stood in the middle of our circle with his close-cropped salt-and-pepper hair and gravelly voice. He looked like a character right out of a war video game in his fatigues. McClure spoke from experience. He had seen action in places like Kosovo and Bosnia.

We set in a circle on the gym floor as McClure addressed the group. We were all prepared to become the next Bruce Lee.

The first thing he said to us was, "Technique barely matters." We were stunned. We'd come there to learn our kicks and thrusts. Charlie Smith, one of my fellow consultants asked, "If technique doesn't matter, what does matter?" McClure replied, "Your head!" He went on to say, "Most people cannot fight because they do not want to, or cannot commit to winning. Fighting is 90% attitude. The good fighters have the mentality."

Thinking that technique is superior, whether in hiring, marketing or selecting an associate is, therefore, a big mistake. Ultimately, technique doesn't really matter. Having worked with literally thousands of people, hundreds of businesses and a thousand dental practices, I can't trace one breakthrough to technique, not one! So choosing a John based on technical competence is unwise.

Underachieving dentists typically look at truly successful practices and wonder, "What management techniques are these practices using?" Dentists constantly ask me, "What business technique do you use to make your client practices so successful?" The answer is "None."

Whatever techniques highly successful practices use are also used by practices that are failing. The most obvious difference is not the techniques being used. The most obvious difference - which is observable within seconds of being in these highly successful practices – is their passion.

That's right, passion. You can feel it just sitting in the reception room. You can feel it when you approach the front desk. You can feel it when you go back down the hall to the operatories. You can feel it when you talk to the dentist in his or her private office. People are passionate about their work.

So when you are recruiting an associate, look for the one who exudes passion. Knowledge gets you into the game. Passion wins it. Like any prospective associate, you won't be able to really tell how excellent he or she is, or how well he or she understands crown and bridge. But what will be palpable at your meeting is his or her passion. People with passion radiate light. They want to do something extraordinary.

Excellence is not easily seen. It often escapes detection. However, the passion for it is unmistakable. And you know it when you see it. Patients, parents, other dentists and staff enjoy being in the presence of genuine passion. Passion is the most critical element in selecting an associate. If a candidate has a passion for dentistry, a passion for excellence, a passion for financial success and a passion for making a difference – you got yourself a great future partner.

PRINCIPAL SIGNS OF PARTNERSHIP PATHOLOGY

My partner of seven years just walked into my office and said he wants out. Why me? Why now?

What a mess this is going to be. I'll need to make sure the non-compete is solid. I'll need to make sure the patients and staff stay with the practice. I'll have to encrypt the data on the computer so he can't get access. I'll need to secure legal counsel immediately. I know I'll end up paying a bundle. I'm really pissed off!

I brought him in eight-and-a-half years ago as an associate. I followed the advice of a well-known consulting company. I spent more than $24K on transition seminars, contracts and other advisors. In the beginning I gave him patients and salary and supported his success. We set up the deal where most of the cost was paid over five years via his production. And this is the thanks I get?

I feel totally blindsided. How did I not see this coming?

o   o   o

Like so many dentists, you were blind to the cardinal signs of partnership pathology. Although the signs were obvious, you preferred to ignore them. These signs are always clear indicators your partnership is headed for the dumpster.

Of course hindsight is 20/20, but I'll bet you had at least one sign, probably more, and simply chose to overlook them. Maybe you thought they were going to be temporary. In any case, it was easier to ignore the signs than to confront them. But when you have even one of these signs, your partnership is heading for trouble. The signs of partnership breakdown are:

- *A Decrease in Communication*

  In the beginning, partners find themselves excited and fully engaged in talking with each other. They are eager to hear what the other has to say. They listen attentively. They share openly. They feel they gain real value from their interactions. They are empowered in their conversations. If these qualities are fading, communication is on the way out. And if your communication is diminishing, it's a sure sign so is your partnership.

- *An Increase in Blame and Criticism*

  If you have repetitive thoughts that blame your partner or are critical of your partner, this is a red flag. If you think he is bugging you or he is annoying you when he walks into the room or when he speaks at your meetings, sirens should be going off. If these thoughts are increasing in frequency, then your partnership is eroding.

  Blame and fault are the antithesis of responsibility. The more you blame your partner and the more you criticize your partner, the less responsible YOU are for the success of the partnership. The more blame and criticism that you have for your partner, the less trust you have in your partner. Blame and criticism also displace acknowledgement and appreciation and partners need to appreciate each other to make it work.

- *A Decrease in Respect*

  In the beginning, there was mutual respect and admiration. You held each other in high esteem. You honored each other. You felt privileged to have each other as a partner.

When you spoke about your partner to colleagues or to your wives, it was always positive. When did it turn negative?

If you find yourself castigating your partner's actions, making him wrong, then respect is disappearing. If you catch yourself losing regard and admiration for your partner, the partnership is headed for trouble.

- *An Increase in Separation*

   In the beginning you used to hang out together. Lunch, after work, even some weekends. If you find yourself making excuses so you don't have to be around your partner, justifying staying apart due to family or other obligations, wake up. More than likely you are in denial that your partnership is headed for danger.

- *Your Focus Turns Inward*

   If you find yourself thinking more and more about "your" situation, wondering about "should have, could have, would have," your focus is being directed inward. If you find yourself continuously revisiting certain upsetting incidents, looking at what you did not do or should have done, and what he did wrong, your focus is turning inward.

   If you find yourself analyzing, judging, assessing or evaluating why the partnership is not working and you are not talking about it with your partner, you are inwardly directed.

   When nearly all your thoughts have "I" or "me" as the subject, you are looking inward. When your thoughts dissect "we" into him or me, your focus is on yourself. You'll never resolve partnership issues focused on yourself.

- *It Feels Like Inequities are Growing*

  If you feel like you're taking on more and more of the business, more of the work load, trouble is brewing. If you feel like you're shouldering more and more of the management responsibilities, the partnership is heading for a crash. If you feel like you are being taken advantage of or your partner is caring less and less, while you are caring more and more, the partnerships has significant problems. If you feel like the bread winner and see your partner as the bread eater, it's time to find out about attorneys.

- *Mutual Initiatives Decrease*

  In the beginning, you had a shared vision. There were things you wanted to accomplish together. Marketing, staffing, equipment upgrades, new procedures – you as a team were going to do so much. Now, each is doing his own thing and there is no shared future, just shared liability, shared overhead, shared staff and shared tasks.

  Partners who don't share a future, who don't work together to make that future happen, do not remain partners.

- *Diminished Aspirations*

  You and your partner were going to have a premier practice. Top of the rank. Best of the best. All those CE courses you were going to take together. All those improvements to the office. Changing staff to get "the right people on the bus." You guys were going to the summit. Now base camp is just fine as long as you make your numbers and fund your retirement.

  Without a shared commitment to a future, the partnership lacks a sufficient context to survive for the long haul. When shared mutual aspirations disappear, so does the glue that holds a real partnership together.

Partnerships do not self-repair. Once they begin to tear, you need to actively mend them. If you had been conscious of these signs of partnership breakdown as they showed up, you would have known to intervene soon as they arrived. Now it's too late.

Oh, by the way, these signs are the same for staff. If these signs show up for a staff member, either fire him or fix it.

PARTNERSHIPS – WHY THEY FAIL

It's been three-and-a-half years since my partner joined my practice. About 11 months ago, he became an owner-partner. Until that time, he was an associate. I thought after almost four years and after becoming a co-owner, he would have become a much stronger leader in the practice. I thought by this time he would be operating with patients as well as I do.

I thought by this time he would have built his side of the practice to be producing at least $50K a month instead of $25K to $30K.

My case acceptance rate is over 80%, his is a little over 50%. I am generating 20 to 25 new patients a month. He's generating about 10. Things are definitely not looking up. His cancellation and no-show rates are much higher than mine and recently we noticed that his collection rate is 5% to 8% lower than mine.

He isn't operating like I expected by this point in time. At staff meetings, he's quiet. He's not out there in the community marketing. He isn't aggressively looking for CE programs to improve his dentistry. He wants to turn everything over to staff rather than talk directly to patients. He's recommending we deliver treatments that require a ton of new equipment, stuff he's heard about but not at all trained in delivering. He's either under- or over-diagnosing. His production is lacking and many days his schedule is not full. Worse, staff members are becoming less and less supportive of him and they are beginning to complain to me about him.

The papers are all signed. I spent about $40K on the entire transition process with a national consulting company. He's paid me a significant down payment for 50% of the practice to purchase over 5 years. This is a disaster! What should I do now?

○   ○   ○

This might sound harsh. But it might be time to confront that you made a mistake and cut your losses.

By the way, you have made one of the most common mistakes made in transitions. And it is the mistake that none of the transition consultants ever talk about. It is this fundamental mistake that costs so many partners their partnership.

Your core values and his core values are not the same!

Whether a partnership in dentistry or in a marriage, when your core values are different, the relationship doesn't work - period.

For example, I'll bet a driving core value of yours is uncompromised patient service. You see the patient as a true customer, someone to be treated special, to be held in high regard. A patient for you is someone who deserves the utmost personal attention by the doctor.

Your partner, on the other hand, likely sees the patient more as an end-user. Some "thing" (not some "one") that can be maneuvered like an object, so it ends up in the right slot at the right time for its dentistry.

You're always concerned about your patients' experience and how it relates to the practice, whereas your partner is much more concerned about delivering the latest technology. Your core values and his are not the same. "Danger, Will Robinson!"

When core values are not aligned between partners, then leadership is always fragmented. Leadership is a verb. Leadership is an action. Leadership is a way of speaking and acting that is consistent with core values. Leadership is an expression of core values. With dissimilar core values, you can't both lead because you lead from one set of core values and your partner leads from another. The result is he stays quiet at staff meetings because he doesn't know what to say to match your speaking. If your partner had similar core values, leadership would be an even, smooth and seamless tag-team effort.

Core values shape how you relate to patients. For you, it's all about having patients honored and respected, listening so they feel appreciated and acknowledged. Given this core value, you'd probably prefer to quote the overall fee. Given this core value, you most likely prefer to ask for the commitment to go through treatment.

For your partner, it's about having the patient managed by staff to accept the treatment plan and all the cool toys to deliver the treatment. So with dissimilar core values, you relate differently to patients. This might explain the difference in case acceptance and marketing.

The same is true for staff. Since you want patients cared for in a particular way as an expression of your core values, you've hired and kept staff that can provide this level of service and caring. Given that you hired these folks, they have known you longer, and they've stayed because their core values and your core values are a match.

So when partners have dissimilar core values, it ends up being disruptive to staff relationships, performance and retention. Although staff members can't put their finger on it, they can sense the core difference between you two and, because they have your core values, they have a difficult time supporting your partner. No wonder they're complaining about him.

What to do?

First, you need to sit down alone and articulate your core values. (Great references are *Beyond Entrepreneurship* by Jim Collins and *The Soul of Business* by Tom Chappell.) You need to be very clear on what your core values are, what they mean and how they shape your perceptions and actions. Have your partner do the same thing. And then meet.

Tell him the partnership is at risk because you have dissimilar core values. Tell him if you can't get on the same page with your core values, you'll have to consider dissolving the partnership.

Present your core values. Have him present his. Where you are in agreement, check it off. Where he is missing your critical and fundamental core values, note them. Make sure he understands what these core values mean to you. Give plenty of examples. Tell him his job is to embody these values and if he can't, it won't work. Give him 90 to 120 days.

What are the odds he'll be able to embody these core values? Slim to moderate. When we talk about core values, we're talking about something that is truly an expression of who one is, and all that goes into oneself – family, culture, religion and upbringing. Usually core values are extremely hard to adopt unless they already live inside you. But give it a shot and see what happens.

By the way, there are no "right" core values. So don't think yours are better than his. They're just different. Your partner's core values may work fine if he practiced solo or with others who held similar core values.

AT-STAKENESS

I am on my second associate and it is going in the same direction as my last one, badly. The associate is a good kid. During the first year, we worked well together through all the documentation: the Letter of Intent, the Appraisal and the Employment Agreement. The Purchase Agreement is now ready for signature. Unfortunately, my associate is not.

I believe I have done everything I could for my associate to succeed. I paid him a good salary for a whole year, gave him patients and let him split hygiene revenues. I also paid for his CE and most of his lab bills and let him order and use dental materials we hadn't used before. I let him do the majority of the hygiene exams to get to know the patients and to schedule any single-tooth undone restorative care. I took him around and introduced him at meetings. I treated him like family.

Nevertheless, after 13 months, his production and new patients are just not enough to make the deal work. He is becoming more removed, less commutative, less committed. This is going the same way as the last associateship – nowhere!

What am I missing?

o   o   o

What's missing? What's missing is you didn't set your associate up to win. You thought by being generous and friendly you would provide an environment where the associate would easily integrate into the practice and produce the necessary marketing and financial results.

Wrong!

What happened is you omitted the most fundamental and critical element for associate success. Without this element in place, the failure rate of associateships skyrockets. This one element incites highly effective action in associates and provokes them to produce top-line and bottom-line results. What is this critical element?

This element is "at-stakeness."

You know what it's like to be "at-stake." Think back. Remember finals week. Remember when you took the Boards. Remember when that restorative project was due on Friday and it was late Thursday night. Remember when you had to make that certain flight. In all these situations you were fully at stake. At-stakeness means you are at stake for the fulfillment of an activity -- or there will be significant consequences if you are unsuccessful.

When you opened your practice, you were fully and wholly at stake: bank notes, rent, supply invoices, legal bills, salary paychecks, new patients – the whole nine yards. If you didn't produce, if you didn't deliver, you would fail. And failure was simply not an option.

At-stakeness produces urgency, increases focus, raises intensity, decreases passivity and enhances the effectiveness of your action. Watching the NBA basketball finals is a very clear demonstration of the at-stakeness phenomenon. With the championship on the line, the level of play on the court is so much more intense and so much better than during the regular season. The more at-stakeness, the higher the level of performance.

In most associateships there is an insufficient level of at-stakeness. The needed condition of at-stakeness is not effectively generated such that the associate's actions produce the required results. If associates were recruited and managed with clear goals, timelines to produce these goals, clear expectations of behavioral outcomes and defined consequences if the goals were not produced, a much higher level of at-stakeness would be generated.

There is typically a cushion practices provide for associates, which sets up a sense of security. In your case, when you began your practice, you had zero security. You were totally at stake. You had to produce or you would fail. In the case of your associate, you've set it up so he doesn't have the same level of urgency, focus, intention or intensity. Why? Because he is not at stake to nearly the same degree you were when you began your practice.

In my coaching, I request that the established dentist generate the following conditions in order to put the incoming associate at stake.

- Generate clear, well-defined and mutually agreed upon goals for the associate. Goals should be set for the first year, broken into months and weeks, sometimes into days, depending on the practice situation. These goals should be in production, collection, new patients, projects that require him or her to manage staff and specific marketing activities.

- Set up a structure to reduce the amount of salary as soon as possible, so as to have him or her get paid mostly from what he or she generates.

- Get a chunk of money down with the stipulation that if he or she fails as an associate, money is lost.

- Operate in the domain of promises and requests. (A request is asking another for a promise.) A promise always puts you at stake. A promise commits you to a future that is not guaranteed. Make promises specific and time-anchored. Negotiate consequences if not fulfilled.

- Mean what you say. Don't be passive-aggressive. Don't back down if he or she underperforms.

Many dentists think that the appropriate documentation and transition facilitation will generate the necessary condition so the associate-to-partner transition works. Well, in my experience, it's like the difference between the menu and the meal. The menu isn't the meal. No matter how well-prepared and elaborate the menu, no matter how well-presented, the menu just isn't the meal. The documents are the menu, and the associate's performance and results in the practice are the meal.

Now if you have the "at-stakeness" conversation with your associate candidate before he or she begins, he or she might say, "No" to your offer. Better now than your saying "please leave" later. If the associate candidate is unwilling to play at stake, then you'll never have a solid partnership, you'll never have someone willing to take the necessary risks to do well or do whatever it takes to have the practice succeed.

A strong level of at-stakeness directly and powerfully impacts the performance of the associate. My advice is: Next time, set it up so the associate is at stake.

DEAL OR NO DEAL

I am about to pull the plug on my associate. He's been here 16 months. I have recurring staff complaints about him, and a few patient complaints, and my wife is starting to complain as well. She's says I am working more, not less. And she's right. With all that's going on, I just don't know if he can make it. I can't see how we can make this a successful partnership.

Sometimes he causes problems and I end up having to clean up his messes. It's not that his numbers are bad. He's consistently making his revenue targets. He's beginning to bring in new patients himself. It's just he's so unaware of the disruptions and bad feelings he sometimes causes.

But I'm reluctant to pull the trigger. I figure I've put over $150K into this deal with the transition consultants, lawyers, appraisers, salaries, hiring more staff, adding equipment and CE. Now at least he's covering his salary and contributing something to the bottom line. And soon the big payoff, where I'll recover my money and then start collecting on 50% of the practice.

Although I've taken more vacation than ever before and have been on call much less, I still don't feel good about it. It isn't that he's a bad kid, but I just can't see how this going to work for the next five to 10 years.

Any advice before I squeeze the trigger?

o   o   o

I would need to spend a lot more time with you and your associate to offer a valid recommendation. But if you're like most associate-to-partnership deals at this stage of the process, more than likely you're going to squeeze that trigger.

In my experience, where the senior partner remains with the practice for a significant period of time and the two parties become equal partners, there comes a critical point in the transition process when the associate and the senior doctor move to the brink of "make or break." This usually occurs somewhere between the first and second year. So you're right on track.

Again, this is only my experience. None of the better-known transition consultancies ever report their long term results in these types of transactions. Why should they? Nobody is asking. They're selling the associate-to-partner product on its merits and it makes them a ton of money. But in my experience, many more fail than succeed.

A failure rarely occurs when the senior doc is selling the practice and leaving quickly or becoming a lame-duck associate, practicing on a very limited basis. I am addressing your circumstance, where the senior doc is staying on as an active co-owner for a period of time.

In your situation, ordinarily 18 months to two years into the associateship, the senior doc starts to experience an emerging reluctance to extend the offer to purchase. The senior doc gets cold feet. He or she perceives the associate isn't ready. Even though the associate is making most or all of his or her production targets and the senior doc has fully recovered his or her production capacity that had slumped for a few months while getting the associate started. So what's the problem?

When you explore the reasons for the senor doc's reticence, it usually comes down to the associate's not thinking, acting or behaving like an "owner."

First, you have to realize that the senior doc has been working in and on the practice for 20 or more years. The level of staff maturity, accountability and performance is very high. Senior staff members know what they're doing. The practice infrastructure, systems and structures are time-tested and reliable. The marketing, whether implicit or explicit, is working and operational. The production and collection numbers are strong, as is the demand for access, as indicated by the long wait time to see the senior doc, along with a robust hygiene schedule.

The senior doc feels tremendous pressure in leading and managing this large, demanding animal. There is less time for vacation. More patients translates into additional clinical, emergency and staff management. More demands. Success has come with a heavy price.

Now add to this consultants proselytizing "optimize your asset value. Reduce your stress. Get a partner. Sell 50% now, 50% later. Take more time off. Be on call less. Make more money and work less. Fund your retirement." Who can resist? Paradise awaits!

What everyone fails to consider is that context is decisive. The practice exists within a context of tenured and proven success. A veteran staff. A well-oiled machine where each part functions at high RPMs. And what goes unrecognized and is rarely addressed is the senior doc has become a highly successful owner. He or she sees the whole picture. They have become competent owners in addition to being competent managers, leaders and marketers. Who they are, the context of their practices, the way the practices operate, is consistent with highly successful owners.

Successful practice owners exist in a different temporality than anyone else in a business, including an associate. Owners have a different set of commitments. Owners have a different array of accountabilities. They clearly understand their unique responsibilities: finding, empowering and keeping the right staff, increasing the operational and negotiable value of the practice and constantly enhancing their relationships with their communities and their patients. The success of their practices is no mistake.

An associate does not have "ownership eyes."

They don't see how one small change they make in the operatory, for example, impacts the front desk, the financial coordinator and the hygienist. They don't see, when they aggressively push a patient toward treatment because their schedule is not full, how it affects the staff and how it looks to the patient. They are blind to what owners see and know.

Senior docs who are successful owners have matriculated and graduated from the school of hard knocks. They know when to keep their mouths shut. They have made and learned from many costly mistakes. This learning has directly impacted the current design of the practice, business and clinical processes. It's why the practice thrives.

So the senior doc looks at the associate and sees someone who rarely appreciates the immense amount of blood, sweat and tears that went into making the practice successful. Someone who doesn't have the slightest idea about how to lead, manage and empower the staff. Someone who doesn't know how to market. Someone who makes rash decisions without consideration of the consequences. And, someone who has cost him or her a lot of time and money. And the thought appears, and recurs on a frequent basis, "Is it worth it?"

The senior doc questions the entire process and sees the associate more as a liability than an asset and the whole relationship begins to unravel. The senior doc decides he or she is better off without the associate. And, like you, he or she slowly squeezes the trigger.

Dentists must accept the fact that partnerships are hard work and require time and patience.

Partnerships require management, leadership and structure. Senior docs need to realize they have to change and this is hard because their success is the product of solo practice. Dentists need to realize this whole deal is a huge commitment. It can work. But first they have to really understand what it takes to be a partner and what it takes to transform a rookie into an All Star player. And if they don't want to do that – if they don't want to invest the time, money and energy – they shouldn't even consider it.

PARTNER VERSUS BUYER

I have recently completed a transition seminar. I've been in practice 24 years and have the kind of practice that seems right for the transition process.

I'm somewhat concerned about entering into this process. I understand what the transition consultants do and how they do it. I understand the process. But what I am not sure about is how to locate and recruit the "right" candidate. Especially because I intend to stay on for another 10 to 12 years.

If I am going to spend all this time and money, who should I be looking for to bring into the practice?

○   ○   ○

Let's get this straight: What you are seeking isn't a buyer, but a partner. A buyer occurs as a short term relationship. You are seeking a partner, which is a long term relationship. Each type of relationship has its own set of characteristics, qualities, commitments and issues. Don't get them confused. Don't make the mistake that thousands of dentists make. Don't let the transition consultant make his $40K at your expense.

If you are looking to sell the practice and exit, then you are looking for someone who has the means to purchase, sees your operation as an opportunity to his or her ends as a solo practitioner and is willing to pay for the assets you have developed over the years. That is called a buyer.

Ultimately, a buyer doesn't care that much about retaining the form and structure of what you have built or retaining the staff you have recruited and maintained – and neither do you, because you are selling it and leaving. When you sell your car to someone, he can paint it any color he pleases.

A buyer wants to assume full ownership, which gives him or her the total rights of ownership. The right to hire and fire. The right to sell the thing to anyone he or she wants. The right to the distribution of the assets (cash). And the right to determine the future of the practice. That means a buyer has no real commitment, no concern, no worry about you after he buys the place. He or she will operate from the point of view that this is a short-term relationship and you soon become yesterday's news.

But you are seeking a partner. A partner is someone who wants to equally share the risk of running the practice. A partner is someone who is as committed to the success of the practice as you. A partner is someone who will work as hard, as long and as urgently as you. A partner is someone who is committed to your success. A partner is someone who will grow the practice beyond your individual capacity to do so. A partner is a long-term relationship. A partner is someone who you feel empowered by, uplifted by and even inspired by. A partner has the same core values, shares the same vision and is gung-ho to achieve the mission. A partner is someone you want to really win and win big. A partner is someone who wholeheartedly appreciates what you have done to build this practice and honors this accomplishment. A partner is someone with whom you can build a future and someone with whom you want to fight your battles. A partner is someone you trust, appreciate and acknowledge.

Finding a buyer is a lot easier than finding a partner. Two factors make finding a partner more difficult. One, most dentists are not great partnership material. There must be a reason that 87% of dentists practice solo and it's been that way ever since the ADA has done its surveys, which has been a long time. Dentists begin and end their training in dental school as an individual achiever. In dental school, it's never about working in teams or partners to achieve a result. The culture of dentistry is based on individual accomplishment. When you think of success in dentistry, you think of individuals. And like you, most dentists have practiced and succeed in solo practice for more than two decades before they decide to take on partners. Having a successful partnership isn't like rolling off a log. If partnerships were easy and produced greater results, many more dentists would already have created them.

The second is there is no proven, tested method for matching senior dentists with compatible younger dentists. I once put together a design team to develop a structured series of online assessments that would successfully match senior dentists looking for dentists with the most compatible dentists coming out of school. Given the pain and turmoil of failed partnerships, given the lack of a national resource, a utility of this nature seemed a no-brainer.

We put together a strong proposal. We went to major suppliers. We went to the largest transition consulting enterprises and dental schools to raise our financing. We went to the ADA. Guess what? The proposal still sits on my shelf. What does that tell you about the political and financial will to make partnerships work?

What the transition consultants aren't telling you is how hard it is to generate and maintain a successful partnership. What they leave out in their transition presentations is how much work it takes in terms of time, commitment and communication to make partnership work. What they leave out is how much of your own money you have to invest to make a partnership succeed. What they avoid telling you is how few of these transitions to partnerships actually make it long-term.

My only advice is to go slowly. Do a lot of due diligence. Hire a good relationship and communication consultant to work with you on selecting a candidate and then work with the candidate to establish your relationship and the structures to work out your concerns. Or, you can do what most do: Sign the documents, pay your cash, roll the dice and hope for the best.

IS IT ME, HIM OR IT?

We're in the beginning of the third year of a transition. I paid a national company to advise and manage the transition process – appraisal, contracts, agreements and financing. The first two years seemed to go pretty well, but now I am running into a few problems.

The problems are not huge, but they are becoming more and more frequent and annoying. Little things are beginning to show up in my associate's management, leadership and marketing.

I called my transition consultant in Southern California. He said that most of the transitions his company does do not have problems. "You are more the exception than the rule." He said these things usually work out well.

I have two questions. Why am I having these problems? How should I address them?

o   o   o

My experience is the complete opposite of your transition consultant's. But my sample is limited to 30 to 40 partnership experiences. And I am usually interacting with dental associateships and partnerships down the road, after the papers have been signed and the transition is two to five years old.

It's no surprise to anyone that transition consultants close the deal and then exit. None of them measure the long-term success of their work. They don't hear about problems because they don't check back. They're onto the next deal, kind of like real estate agents. In my view, all partnerships, and I mean all, have problems.

You can't solve problems unless you admit they exist. And partnerships always have problems. It's inevitable. It's predictable. If you have a partnership, you have problems. Problems come with the territory.

Partners are human. Humans are imperfect. You have two people, two personalities, two psychologies, often generational differences, familial differences and cultural differences, all in the heat of operating a business where risks are high and pressures are intense.

Because partners are imperfect and because all partnerships have problems, partnerships should regularly schedule ongoing exercises to handle their inevitable problems and improve their effectiveness as partnerships. Unfortunately, in dentistry, few do.

If dentists knew they should expect problems, it might create havoc for many transitions consultants. But failing to recognize that partnerships invariably have problems sets up potential partners for great disappointment.

If you expect partnerships to be problem-free, and then you have problems, the only conclusion you are left with is something is wrong. Something is wrong with your partner. Something is wrong with you. Something is wrong with the transition consultant. Or something is wrong with the practice that it cannot support a partnership. When problems are unexpected, the only conclusion is something is wrong.

Thinking something is wrong with your partnership, your practice or yourself leads to behaviors and actions that damage the partnership, usually resulting in the partnership falling apart or each partner operating as an independent operator.

What would it be like if everyone entering into a partnership knew from the get-go that there would be problems? What if both parties knew from the beginning the particular problems they could expect to have as their associateship-to-partnership unfolded?

What if transition consultants wrote this equation in their contracts: *Partnerships = Problems (Always)*? What if everyone agreed you need to figure out a solid structure and a consistent model of communication to address and resolve these partnership problems? What kind of difference would that make? It would make a very big difference!

In my work, there are three domains I ask associates and partners to engage in, confront and act on. First, dentists need to understand that they are poor communicators. It's one of the reasons they sought dentistry as a profession in the first place. Dentistry is a structural vocation. You work with your hands, not your lips. Add to this that dentists are extremely conflict-averse and any situation that hints of conflict is avoided.

As a consultant and coach, I spend time with partners, teaching and training them on how to communicate their issues, expectations and concerns. I work with them on how to directly bring up and handle conflict. If not handled, these issues, expectations, concerns and conflicts increase in mass and intensity until they turn into irresolvable breakdowns.

We begin their training by teaching them how to communicate expectations and concerns. We use a proven model of how to determine and then how to satisfy their partner's expectations and how to uncover and then resolve the other's concerns. We insist they have routine, scheduled partnership meetings that always include addressing each other's expectations and concerns.

Transition consultants don't set dentists up to expect their passage to be problem-free, they just don't address the partnership issues that will inevitably arise. If a smooth partnership occurs, it's pure luck. Better to count on your partnership having problems from the get-go, so you won't be upset when they happen – because they will. It is better to learn how to work out your problems with your partner than to expect not to have them.

Another equally important area where I observe partnership fractures is in dealing with how to make decisions. The senior partner has been making decisions for 20 years. The junior partner often feels left out and impotent, as all decisions are unquestionably made by the senior dentist. That's what the senior dentist is used to, that's what has worked in the past, that's what has produced the results that can afford a partner in the first place. So, any time a problem arises, whom does the staff go to?

We have developed a model based specifically on decision-making by policy. In this process, the partners act like a Board of Directors of a corporate entity. It works brilliantly. When decisions are made by policy, not on personality or seniority, things get handled without resentment or righteousness.

So, if you are considering entering into a partnership, understand you will have problems. Figure out your models and structures to consistently and directly address your problems, so when they arise, and they will arise, you get them handled.

My advice to you is to get an adviser and sit down with your associate. Put the problems on the table so they aren't around the table or under the table. And then get your problems addressed and resolved – because they won't go away.

HOW DO YOU CHOOSE A TRANSITION CONSULTANT?

I am ready to make the move to recruit an associate and over time convert him or her to being a partner. I've attended three programs from different consulting groups and each seems to have a different yet similar approach to the process. How do I know which one is best for me?

○   ○   ○

Most dentists haven't a clue about how to manage consultants or advisers. It was quite a wake-up call for me when I began to consult in other industries, with a few major companies like Boeing, Intel and GE Capital. These companies were very rigorous and demanding in having me state specifically what outcomes I would produce and by when I would deliver them and in requiring me to list my tasks and timelines. Then they'd tie part of my compensation to the results produced. So I suggest you do the same thing. Make sure you have the consultant clearly define what he or she will deliver (results and outcomes) and the consequences if he or she doesn't deliver.

Unfortunately, most transition consultants are like car salesmen: When you drive the car off the lot, it's not their problem any more. I only know one transition consultant who really follows up downstream to make sure the partnership is working. So if you can, see if your transition consultant is willing to put something at stake in the contract, particularly if the partnership doesn't work out. My bet is he or she will dance around this one, but it's worth a shot.

Most transition consultants will take you through the same process. What follows is an edited transcript of a conversation I had with one of the premier transition consultants in the dental industry, Dr. Tom Ziegler.

Over the last five years, I have worked with a number of transition advisers and consultants. Dr. Ziegler and I have worked collaboratively many times. Tom consistently has delivered time after time and been highly responsive and, most important, he keeps his word.

Given Tom's background of experience, knowledge and success, I talked to him about his perspective on putting these deals together. I wanted someone who could explain to dentists the steps and required documents in the associateship-to-partnership process. Plus I wanted his insights on what makes partnerships fail.

Dr. Tom Ziegler practiced orthodontics for over a decade before returning to school to become an attorney. Tom acknowledges that his major influence and inspiration was Harvey Sarner, chief legal counsel for the American Dental Association. Sarner helped many dentists realize the importance of incorporation, retirement plans and tax savings. Tom first met Harvey while he was in dental school and was so impressed with his efforts to help dentists that he attended most of his seminars over the next 10 years.

MBC: Why did you tailor your law career to the practice-transition process for dentists?

Tom: Ten years ago, 3M UNITEK asked me to develop a course outline to help orthodontic residents with tax issues and to help them with Associate Employment Agreements and purchases of existing practices.

It was through my experience with those residents that I realized that there were only a handful of firms working in that area and I thought there was a need.

MBC: How would you evaluate the transition process and the transition consultant to know if he or she knows what he or she is doing?

Tom: Generally speaking, transition consultants familiar with the processes do practice transition full-time. Therefore, they will generally have been in business for a while and will have references that can be contacted and queried.

Word of mouth marketing is best. Ask those who have recently taken on an associate or partner or those who recently purchased a practice. Was the consulting process fair and was it easy, fast and reasonably priced?

Interview the consultant you are considering. Establish for yourself how accessible this person will be, how much experience he or she has and whether he or she will be willing to tailor the plan to your needs – and, above all, whether the consultant has the ability and patience to explain things to you.

MBC: What's wrong with a handshake deal?

Tom: I think simplicity appeals to most of us. What would be simpler than, "Come work for me for X amount of money and if it works out, I'll sell you part of my practice and we'll be partners"?

The problems with that simplicity are many. None of the potential problems that could arise have been raised, discussed or resolved. Specificity leads to understanding. Simplicity is too vague.

MBC: What do you say to a dentist who says, "I'm almost positive I want this person as a partner, but I will not know for sure until we work together for a while. Therefore, I don't want to go to the effort and expense of creating a document that may never be used"?

Tom: It is precisely because the potential partnership might not work out that we need documents that specify the remedies if it does not.

MBC: What remedies are you referring to?

Tom: A remedy comes up in, "What if this does not happen? Then what?" The "what" is the remedy. Issues that need remedies include notice. How much notice must I give you if I want to quit, or how much notice must you give me if you want to fire me? What if I don't give you the required notice? Then what?

If I'm required as an employer to give my employee 90 days' notice, the remedy might be that I have to pay him or her for 90 days after I provide termination notification. If I'm required to give 90 days' notice as an employee, the remedy would be I have to work those 90 days or pay damages to the employer, something along the lines of 90 days' pay.

MBC: In addition to remedies for notice, what other issues might come up?

Tom: Restrictive covenants are a list of things the employee cannot do if he or she leaves the practice, such as soliciting patients from the former practice. You cannot take patient lists and contact them. Hiring away current employees is also a no-no.

Developing proprietary information is a restriction.

Opening a competing practice within a specified area for a specific amount of time, commonly called a "covenant not to compete," is important. The remedies spell out what the consequences of violating the covenants are.

For example, if I hire one of your employees away, I will pay you $50K compensation.

If I solicit your current patients, I will pay you $5K per patient taken.

If I open a competing practice within the restricted area, I will pay you 30% of my gross income for the duration of the restriction.

MBC: What other specifics that might be lacking in a handshake deal should a dentist be concerned about?

Tom: I think dentists should not re-invent the wheel. They should take advantage of the experience of thousands of practice transition deals in determining an appraisal of the practice as well as in establishing the contents of Associate Employee Agreements and Purchase and Sale Agreements. Lawyers who work in the area of dental practice transition have accumulated a list of all of the potential or real problems that can come up and have entered them as new sections in such agreements.

MBC: Are you saying a good agreement is specific to dentistry and is basically a laundry list of all known, real problems that have come up with other dentists in the past?

Tom: Yes. A good agreement will contain a complete list of possible problems and appropriate solutions. Therefore, the dentist who fears that the deal might not go through will know in advance what will happen if it does not.

MBC: Tell me about the process. Where does it begin?

Tom: I begin the process by asking the senior dentist and the junior dentist to each separately compose a wish list and send it to me confidentially. I want to know what each dentist wants or thinks he or she wants to happen. I want each dentist to be open and completely honest without the fear of offending a potential partner.

MBC: What information do you want on your wish lists? What are you looking for?

Tom: I ask the dentists to write down as much as they can think of that they would want if they were king. Don't hold back. The purpose, of course, is to learn what the expectations of each dentist are and to determine which ones can be granted and to ferret out where the potential conflicts live and work in resolving those areas.

MBC: In your experience, how many partnerships fail?

Tom: I have heard some large failure percentages thrown around at various dental meetings – but most of the people quoting those numbers aren't even in the practice transition business. In my own experience, working with consultants like you who work on the relationship end, over the past 10 years of being involved with hundreds and hundreds of practice transitions, I have only seen a handful break up.

MBC: Well, I know that every client with whom we have collaborated has succeeded. You bring a particular set of elements and distinctions to the entire process that is very effective.

Tom: Yes, the process we use has a strong track record of success. We certainly have potential partnerships that don't go to inception. I have not bothered to keep statistics on the exact percentage of dentists who have contacted me and ended their relationship prior to completion of documents.

MBC: Can you describe what you mean by "the process"?

Tom: Generally speaking, the process is to put forward all potential conflicts and to discuss them and work out solutions ahead of time. Our goal is to leave nothing to chance.

The obvious areas to identify and resolve are what the overall plan is and what the remedy is if it doesn't work out. The process involves a series of questions and answers to determine if the positive goals are compatible.

MBC: After you have the wish lists, what is the next step?

Tom: The next step is completing an appraisal of the current value of the practice. That not only establishes the value of the practice, but the amount to be paid for a share of that practice. Depending on the size of the practice, various methods and procedures become available for purchase options.

MBC: In your appraisal, do you include suggestions for purchase options?

Tom: Yes. I believe that part of the appraisal process is not only establishing the price to be paid, but also determining how the price allocations will be made that affect taxes and how financing will be done. I think those basics are needed for both sellers and buyers to evaluate what they will be receiving or what they will be paying. This is the first significant document upon which agreement must be reached.

MBC: Assuming both sides are comfortable with the appraisal, what is the next step?

Tom: The next step is really in two parts. One is an Associate Employment Agreement and the other is the Purchase and Sale set of agreements.

MBC: Can you give me some idea of what information should be contained in the Associate Employment Agreement?

Tom: Beginning and ending dates.

          Amount of compensation.

          List of employee benefits in addition to compensation – including pension, malpractice insurance premiums, dues and license expenses, health insurance premiums, travel, continuing education and automobile and disability or life insurance expenses – as well as who pays for each of those items.

          List of duties.

          List of staff and facilities available to employee.

          Statement of employment or list of exceptions.

          Explanation of who determines fees.

List of vacation, sick and CE days.

List of holidays.

Section on accelerating the sale of the practice if the employer dies during the employee's Employment Agreement and before the closing date of the sale.

List of restrictive covenants, such as non-competition time and distance, non-disclosure of information terms and rules for not inducing employees to leave.

List of remedies for breach of a covenant.

Determination of where notices are to be delivered.

List of governing laws of venue (location) that apply to dispute resolution.

Statement that if employment agreement is terminated, then agreement for purchase and sale is voided as well.

Definition of terms in termination section, including "without notice," "automatic" and "with cause."

Arbitration section pointing out that all disputes will be resolved by arbitration rather than lawsuit.

MBC: What kinds of documents are involved in the Purchase and Sale Agreement?

Tom: The basic agreement is for the purchase and sale of stock where a functional (less than 100%) sale of a professional corporation is involved -- or purchase and sale of a partnership interest in the case of an unincorporated practice.

The agreement sets forth "how, when, for how much and how you get paid" regarding the fractional transfers. For example, "I will sell you 50 shares of the 100 issued and authorized shares of my PC representing a 50% interest at the rate of 10 shares each year for five years, and you personally will pay me personally $10K per year for those shares by certified check on January 2 each year. New share certificates in the amount of 10 for you and 90 for me will be reissued. Your shares will be held in escrow until all 50 are paid for."

MBC: What agreements affect day-to-day operations?

Tom: Once the buy-in has begun on the closing date, the corporation has more than one shareholder, so there needs to be a shareholders' agreement. The shareholders' agreement describes how stock may be transferred and under what events – death, disability, retirement, corporate dissolution – and how much and under what terms payment will be made for each event.

MBC: What about a statement of expectations or conditions of satisfaction?

Tom: I think there cannot be too much specificity written down as to the understanding between the parties. That can be attached as an addendum to the shareholders' agreement.

MBC: Do the shareholder dentists need new Employment Agreements between themselves and the PC?

Tom: Yes. New Employment Agreements are required containing the restrictive covenants. Also, it is frequently within those agreements that we make adjustments to compensation that pays the majority of the purchase price through income differential between the parties before W-2 income is tabulated.

The buy-in method benefits the buyer; therefore, we set up the buy-out to benefit the seller. The purchase price would be for the balance of the stock and all of the seller's personal goodwill payable in cash through third-party financing at the closing of the second 50%.

MBC: How much of the money paid in during the buy-in years before would be paid back if the parties split?

Tom: That leads us to the final supplemental agreement. It governs the buy-in period before the parties are 50/50 partners. Basically, if the buyer quits, he or she gets half the money back that he or she paid in for stock and through income differential. It gets paid back as deferred compensation payable over a five-year period. On the other hand, if the employer fires the employee, the employee gets all of the money he or she paid in for stock and income differential, payable in cash within 30 days.

MBC: How are assets split if the buy-in is completed and the two are 50/50 partners and they decide then to split?

Tom: All of those remedies would be articulated in the Purchase and Sale basic document.

Once they are 50/50 partners, no one can get fired. But if one partner wants out, the senior partner retains the right to keep the office and buy out the junior partner for half the then-re-appraised value of the practice. Or the senior partner may elect to sell his half interest for that amount and leave subject to the restrictive covenants.

MBC: When do the dentists first see the Associate Employment Agreement, the Purchase and Sale Agreement, the shareholders' agreement, the new Employment Agreements and the supplemental agreement?

Tom: Within a month or so after we have basic agreement on the appraisal, including a Letter of Understanding, we draft and supply to both parties first drafts of all documents.

MBC: What is the purpose of the first drafts?

Tom: They are working documents used to focus the three of us – lawyer, buyer and seller – on all of the potential issues.

We are asking for changes, deletions, additions and clarifications that the parties want.

This is where partnership is formed or terminated before anything has been signed.

Our goal is to end up with no surprises.

MBC: I mentioned conditions of satisfaction before. Maybe you should address them now.

Tom: Sure. Whereas with marriage, children and God, commitments are unconditional, in business, commitments are always conditional. In other words, in business, certain conditions need to be present for people to make and keep commitments. For example, a front desk can't make a commitment to a certain level of production unless there are a sufficient number of patients available to schedule.

In an associateship or a partnership, there are numbers of commitments that need to be made – to particular behaviors, to certain actions and to specific results. In fact, your documents spell out the commitments pretty clearly.

What conditions are required for each party to make and keep the commitments? For example, a new associate is committed to a certain collection target after six months. But without a condition of support by the senior dentist in speaking effectively to his patients about the younger doctor doing their dental work, the associate can never fulfill that commitment.

Conditions can vary from communication to operations to revenue generation. For example, in communication, conditions such as straight talk, no nonsense and honest communication are conditions often established. Then there are the conditions needed for operational commitments, such as actively marketing the practice and attending community groups, such as Rotary Club meetings, to generate new patients.

Once we articulate the conditions of satisfaction, we convert them into agreements – and then the agreements are added to the documents in the form of an addendum where a signature is required.

Defining and agreeing to the conditions of satisfaction has been a fabulous tool to pre-empt most of the problems, issues and breakdowns in associateships and partnerships.

MBC: Given your background of experience, and seeing what works and what doesn't, what would you say are the areas in a partnership relationship that provide the greatest likelihood of becoming problems?

Tom: I see 15 potential partnership relationship problem areas.

<u>Vastly Different Personality Types</u>

The statement that opposites attract does not apply to a happy partnership.

Although it is true that each partner has his or her own set of strengths and that each partner's strengths could compliment the other partner's weaknesses, the more similar partners are in their core values, their work ethic, their vision and how they deal with people in general, the better the relationship.

<u>The Workaholic and the Person Who Wants to Take a Lot of Time Off</u>

Each partner must express his desire and come to an agreement on what is acceptable. Both the issues of compensation and authority to run the practice day to day need to be raised when one partner is in the practice significantly more than the other.

<u>The Neat Freak and the Pig Pen</u>

Compulsively neat people will eventually resent messy people. This seemingly trivial difference can be a festering irritant.

<u>Playing Favorites with Staff</u>

Partners who gossip or attempt to become the more popular partner with staff members are very divisive and cause disruption to the office.

Partners must confide in each other out of ear shot of staff and maintain a united front with staff.

Inter-spousal Relationships

Ideally, partners and their spouses would socialize and enjoy each other's company. However, when a partner has complained to his or her spouse regarding something the other partner has done, rather than confronting the other partner to resolve it, spouses will side with their mates and carry that resentment into the social arena.

Incompatible Practice Image and Direction

Partners need to agree on what image the practice should project and how that image will be nurtured and maintained.

This involves equipment, décor, website, stationery and uniforms. One may want to expand and grow bigger, while the other may want to maintain a boutique practice.

Disagreement over Office Hours

Partners need to share the unpleasant early morning, evening or Saturday hours as evenly as possible.

Nitpicking

A partner must be willing to work 51% of the time for 49% of the pay. You cannot count paperclips or think you are working more than your slacking partner. You have to be willing to accept that without concern.

Lack of Comfort Level with Aggressiveness of Quasi-Personal Tax Write-off through the Practice

My solution is addressed in our documents wherein each partner can write off any expense against his or her portion of the net income as long as he or she indemnifies the other partner.

Treatment Philosophies Are Not Compatible

Treatment philosophies need to be compatible or they can lead to problems. One partner cannot want a denture mill and the other a crown and bridge practice.

Fee Schedules Need to be Compatible

One cannot want to advertise $200 dentures and the other charge $200 for an exam and prophy.

Expectations Not Met

I know you spend a great deal of time working with partnerships in addressing expectations and concerns. This is really a tremendous benefit. As you always say, unfulfilled expectations lead to upsets. And upsets unexpressed cause discomfort and ultimately dissolution of the partnerships. I appreciate how you train partners to articulate exactly what is expected and teach them how to convert these expectations into negotiated requests.

One Partner's Spouse is Office Manager

If a spouse of a partner is in charge of office finances, the other partner might feel at a disadvantage. This leads to suspicions, and extra care needs to be demonstrated to include the non-spouse partner in all financial data.

Lack of Communication

Again, this is one area that I know you work with partners on – how to effectively communicate. In my experience, this is the greatest source of partnership failure – bar none. Failure to take time to talk, to really communicate with each other on a daily basis, is costly. Speak the unspoken. Talk about the mole hill before it becomes a mountain.

Lack of a Desire to Please Your Partner

Failure to genuinely attempt to please your partner – to do more than your fair share. If you don't care about your partner's success, well-being and happiness, it will show up as feelings of "He is taking advantage of me. He is not doing his fair share. He doesn't care about it as much as I do." If you don't want your partner to really win, if you're unwilling to support and empower him or her, then it becomes a lose-lose game. Adhere to the Golden Rule.

MBC: Tom, thanks for your time and our partnership over these past few years. The success of our clients is outstanding and a lot has to do with your good work.

THINKING & ACTING LIKE A BOARD OF DIRECTORS

I have been in a partnership for six years. But it's more like two independent practices than a partnership. We definitely avoid the big issues, avoid making tough decisions and are afraid to cause a conflict. Both of us would probably do just as well practicing by ourselves.

You often suggest setting up the partnership as a Board of Directors. I see this as a real solution to our situation. But I still don't quite understand how this process works. Could you explain it in much greater detail?

○   ○   ○

The best way to answer your question is for me to present a recent interview I did with one of my collaborative consulting partners, Mr. Art Haines. We deliver a program – *The Partnership Governance Program* – that is designed to educate, train and develop partners to be effective Directors of their Boards.

MBC: Art, what exactly is governance?

Art: Governance – or the purpose of governance – is to assure that the resources of your practice, such as the people, facilities, equipment and money, are deployed in a way that maximizes the benefit that you, as the owner, want from the practice.

There are a couple of words that are pretty critical in that definition. First of all, it says "deploy." We're not saying "doing." Governance is not about the doing of your practice. It's about deploying your resources in such a way that they help you achieve what you want from the practice.

The second word that's very important is "benefit." It really implies that part of governance is defining what you as the owner want to get out of that practice. That's the purpose of governance. It's to ensure that your resources are organized, managed and monitored in such a way that you get the benefits out of the practice that you want.

MBC: How is governance different from what I do on a day-to-day basis?

Art: We believe that every dentist owner wears three hats when he or she walks into his or her practice. First, the provider is a worker or a doer. He or she is a key part of the team that's driving production, the economic engine of your practice.

Secondly, the provider is a manager. He or she organizes the practice resources on a day-to-day and week-to-week basis to make sure that the operation is running smoothly.

Third, the dentist is an owner. He or she owns the practice. And if he or she is like 99% of professionals, the work and the everyday management of the practice covers most of what he or she does – leaving very little time for owning and governing.

Most of what you may be doing by way of governance right now is *thinking* about the direction of your practice and the benefits you want to get out of it.

That's usually done on an informal, implicit basis. In the *Partnership Governance Program*, we've placed heavy emphasis on written policies, where the decisions of governance are written down so the practice staff can consistently apply them. That's particularly important to you as the owner as you work with your staff and partners. When it's all said and done, that's probably the biggest visible difference, the emphasis on enough formality and structure that you end up with a written record of your governance decisions.

MBC: What difference can governance make in a small practice – or in any dental practice?

Art: We have found that a lot of dentists feel like their practices are controlling them and they want to get back in control. It's real common to hear dentists say they really never get to the big issues. They never get to the concerns about where they're going with their practices and whether their practices are really doing what they want them to do.

Governance can make a difference there. In fact, one of the key issues in governance is really getting control of your practice and taking it in the direction that you want it to go.

The other area that we see a lot of governance implications in is partner relationships. If the partnership's not going well, it can generate a lot of conflict that has to be dealt with. And this requires an inordinate amount of time and energy. Governance can actually improve that process, making it more efficient and less stressful.

Many dentists and their partners want to expand their practices to bring in new partners. But they're unsure about how to do it in a way that's going to be successful. They may actually feel blocked in doing that. Governance can make a big difference there in expanding the practice and bringing in new partners.

MBC: You talk about how governance can help dentists with the feeling that their practices are controlling them, rather than vice versa. And you talk about how governance can reduce conflicts and improve energy. Further, you tell us that governance can expand a practice's capacity to generate successful additions to the partnership. How does that work? How does governance help produce those results?

Art: We find with dental practices that two things typically occur. One, they rely a lot upon personal relationships to try to get things done. Every time they come up against a problem, it's like the first time they've encountered and tried to deal with it. They end up re-fighting or rehashing issues over and over again.

        Too many practices never get to the place where the partners reach agreement on things and move forward. The thing that written policies do for you is force you to start achieving consistency. You've got a record of what you've agreed upon. That comes into play when something comes up – like an opportunity, a problem or a conflict.

        You can use written policies as a basis to say, "Here's how we said we were going to decide this. Here's what we decided the last time. Now let's move forward from this point." You end up putting less emotional energy into dealing with last year's problems and more energy into deciding where you want to go.

MBC: So if a practice or a partnership institutes governance through policy, what results can it expect?

Art: At the most basic level you should sleep easier at night knowing you've established a direction for your practice. It's been documented specifically how you're going to deal with problems and issues through processes and procedures.

It's a less stressful way of going about your business and one in which working with your current and new partners takes less of an emotional toll. With governance rules firmly in place, you can get back to running your practice. You're setting the direction and you have a management system for getting there. You know the results you want and you have a structure for achieving them.

MBC: Let's go a little deeper on that one. How do you put yourself back at the helm? How does that work?

Art: We'll talk about the five questions of governance a little bit later. But one of the very first questions of governance is, "What's your vision for your practice?" in very concrete terms. Where do you see your practice five years from now? What are the values you'll use to make decisions?

That's the essence of being at the helm. You'll have a very clear structure for managing the day-to-day operations of your practice. You will know who's responsible for what and what his or her accountability is. In fact, you'll be back on track to get from here to your vision.

MBC: If I'm a dentist, and everything's going well, why should I care about governance? I'm making money. The income is going up. I'm happy with my practice. Why should I care about governing?

Art: My first question is whether you have a clear vision of where you want to be five years, three years or even two years from now. It's one thing to be very happy right now. It's quite another to be on track for where you want to go.

One of the things we know about dental practices is at the core of their businesses the only thing that is certain these days is change. Governance is going to put you in a better position to chart a course for the future and deal with the inevitable changes in this business called "dental practice."

Another question for you is whether you have partners right now. Are you looking to expand your practice with additional partners, either to start cashing out your position as the sole owner or to expand the asset value of the practice?

If you want partners, have you had success in creating partners in the past and do you know how to create success in the future with them? Governance can be very helpful in assisting you in making that kind of change in your practice.

MBC: What are the signs that I should be looking for to know that I need to install a governance function in my practice?

Art: Well, I think of them in three areas. We've already talked about one. That is the sense of being out of control or constantly in a short-term crisis mode – or being controlled by your practice.

Another is the whole issue of a strained or ineffective relationship with your partner. Where there is a strained or ineffective relationship with your partner, you'll often find a lot of conflict. Conflict takes far too much energy to generate meaningful and effective output. If conflict is increasing, you are absolutely headed for a failed partnership or associate relationship.

The third – and this one is obvious – is poor practice performance. The tendency when we've got a practice that's not performing well, either in the marketplace or operationally, is to push harder and harder on day-to-day operations. In fact, the overall direction and structure of the practice at the highest level, at the ownership level, may actually be the most important problem to be dealt with.

MBC: If my practice is a mess right now, can governance help me turn it around?

Art: Yes, but it's still not a panacea. We ought to be honest about this. It can certainly help you focus on the right problems, which will then allow you to start working on them. That's from both a short-term and a long-term perspective. One thing good governance will do is help you identify the new competencies you're going to need to get your practice out of the stew.

MBC: Could you explain that in a little more depth?

Art: The supposition here is the practice is a mess. It could be you don't have good competency either in your day-to-day management of the practice or your leadership of the practice and the direction you're moving it in isn't strong. That may keep you from uniting your staff around a common mission.

Actually, those are very different competencies, one's day-to-day management and one's long-term leadership and direction. Through the governance process, you'll start uncovering where those issues are. You'll be able to focus on where you or your staff needs to develop new skills. Frankly, you may discover where you need to change some staff to get the right skills to get your practice out of the mess.

MBC: It allows you to see or perceive the practice differently and gives you access to activities or actions that you would not have seen otherwise?

Art: Exactly.

MBC: So if I were a dentist, what would I need to do to begin the process?

Art: I think the first decision is an internal one: Make a commitment to retake the helm of your practice. So often practices are on autopilot, with the owner coming in every day and dealing with the crisis or problem of the moment. On autopilot, you stay focused on what this year's income is going to be – but you don't make the commitment of time and mental energy required to take the helm of your practice and move into the future. That is what you really want for your practice.

Second, once you've made the mental decision to take the helm of your practice, you must seriously address the five questions of governance that we will be talking about. Take it on as a regular part of your professional and personal life. It is, indeed, a life's work. That holds true until you retire from the practice of dentistry.

Also, you'll probably need to seek assistance from an adviser to understand practice governance. Unfortunately, there are not many out there who really understand governance in its application to small professional practices. But it's very helpful. We certainly find with our program that moving people through the process offers a lot in the way of assistance in this domain.

MBC: What if we don't have an idea about the future the way you're talking about it? What if we don't have a strategic plan?

Art: Let me respond with something that's maybe both obvious and not obvious. Ownership always precedes strategy. Taking ownership of your practice becomes the reason for creating a strategy.

As owner of your practice, the first question has to do with your vision for the future, in very concrete terms, and the values that you'll use to make your decisions. That is the cornerstone of any strategic plan.

Actually, what we say is by taking ownership and the helm of your practice and answering the question of vision and values, you've taken the first big and important step in strategic planning.

Based, then, on your vision, values and where you want to take your practice, you may need a very detailed strategic plan or a simple, not terribly detailed one.

It really depends upon your direction, the guidance of your practice and where you want to take it with your vision and values. The short answer to your question is you actually don't need a strategic plan to start down the road of governance. The first step of governance is to create that cornerstone for your strategy.

MBC: What is the downside and what are the risks of defining a governance structure? What's the risk on my side if I'm an owner of a practice?

Art: By definition, this is a change. Change can always be threatening and risky when you're working with people, both staff and others. There are also some risks to your partner relationships if you uncover difficult issues that you need to work through.

In employee relationships, when you start to make expectations and outcomes much more explicit and when you change the direction of your practice, there's risk there too.

Frankly, the specificity of written policies may be threatening to some who prefer to work in an environment that's not as specific, but a little more open-ended.

One big risk is that you won't be successful with governance and that it won't make a difference in your practice for whatever reason. You can hedge those risks by keeping the end in mind.

When you're clear about your vision for the future and you make sure to keep that in mind, you'll create the right kind of governance to get there. If you move carefully, in pace with the amount of change that you, your partners and your practice can absorb, you can avoid the risks of too much change too quickly. Just pay careful attention to the skills you need to make governance work.

Typically, good communication skills and good conflict resolution skills – and, often, a modicum of business planning and objective-setting skills – are important. As you run into barriers in moving forward with governance in the management of your practice, keep your eyes open for where you need to see consistency and secure some additional expertise in those areas.

MBC: You've carried people through the process several times. What would you consider to be the kinds of stages dentists go through to start it – and then come out of it? What do you see happening in that process for those guys?

Art: For anybody to undergo the process there is an initial interest and excitement about what it can do. As we walk people through, there's a confrontation with the fact that some of the questions are a little difficult. We need to think some things through.

MBC: Give some examples of some of the tougher questions that dentists have to confront.

Art: If you have not, as partners, sat down and discussed where you see your practice five years in the future or if you're a solo practitioner and you have never really thought about specifically where you want your practice to be five years in the future, doing so can sound very attractive, theoretically. But when you sit down to work it through, frankly, it can require a lot of emotional and mental energy.

It can involve some pretty frank, candid discussions between partners if they've not looked at emerging issues, particularly if you've got partners with different stages of family formation or partners who are already looking towards retirement.

The five-year vision for a young dentist just out of school and looking to pay off debts might be different than the vision for an older dentist on the verge of retirement. That's a great example.

Another one is what the benefits are that I want from my practice in addition to good, solid income. You can bump right up against different value structures right out of the box.

Why would you want to do that? So you can reach some alignment and begin to work together to create a practice that creates the benefits that you as a group of partners want to achieve. That's the best mix of the affected parties' interests. You can move forward on that goal and avoid the conflicts of constantly bumping up against different value structures and needs for the future that you've never even put on the table and talked about.

MBC: What happens if my partner and I can't reach agreement on important issues?

Art: I think it's interesting to reflect on what happens right now. I'll bet that if you can reach easy agreement, the issues are usually avoided until they become crises. It's at that point that you either solve them grudgingly, under pressure, or the practice starts to fall apart.

Under a governance structure, one of the questions that we ask dentists to talk about is how they'll make decisions. Are you going to do it by vote or by consensus? Do senior partners have a veto? Be very explicit about how and by whom decisions are made. Begin to work through how you will manage conflict when it comes up or what you'll do when you're at loggerheads.

In our work with dentists, we spend a fair amount of time on the communication and conflict management skills that will support the whole policy structure. Whatever conflict management and communication skills you have right now will be made all the more effective by documenting an effective decision-making process.

It's not a cure-all, but it will make running the practice easier by having the process written down. Then, under pressure and stress, you have a system and process that you can fall back on to help you move through some of the difficult issues.

MBC: What are the risks if a staff refuses to accept the fact of a governance approach?

Art: It really depends upon your staff. We find that staff members who are results-oriented and who really want to work in a practice that's moving forward to some vision for the future and that has clear accountabilities may actually be frustrated because they're not doing so now. And they will thrive working under a governance kind of approach.

Those who sort of like to hide behind confusion and the lack of clarity won't like it and will likely leave. It's certainly one of the outcomes of good governance. You may lose some of your staff because it's just not the kind of system that they want to work under.

MBC: What is involved in defining practice governance?

Art: We believe that it's writing down thoughtful and detailed answers – also known as "policies" – to five questions. The first question is "What are the vision and values that will guide every decision in your practice?" We find that dentists who take it seriously by defining a vision and values for the future refer back to them and use them as a basis for decision-making when they hit the tough obstacles. It really is a big step forward in the issue of taking the helm of your practice.

The second question is "What benefits will the practice create for you, the owners of the practice?" That involves moving beyond simply saying, "Yearly income." You need to look at issues such as time off, professional development, relationships, balanced family life and community service. What are the benefits that you care about in addition to income that you want the practice to generate?

The third question is "How will we govern the practice?" You need to decide who will be participating in governance decisions and discussions. Is it just the owners? Full partners? Do employees and associates have a seat at the table? Do just key employees have a seat at the table? If so, what will their role be in decision-making? This is one that most dentists give a fair amount of consideration to. They recognize that generally it's not just the partners who you want to participate in the governance discussion.

The fourth question is "Who will manage the practice and what is he or she to accomplish?" This is looking at the question of who's accountable for the day-to-day and month-to-month management of the practice and of what his or her objectives are. You also need to determine how you will measure the practice manager's performance.

This is where we ask, once we have defined, as owners, the benefits that we want and our vision for the future, who we charge with creating that future. What are the objectives that person will have in the short run that will move us toward our long-term vision?

The fifth question is "What's the authority that we will delegate to our managers?" Will it include, for example, spending authority? Hiring and firing authority? Staff evaluation authority? What can they do and what can't they do without coming back to the owners?

Those are the five questions of practice governance – but they're not the only five. Typically, when we go through the process with dentists, issues will come up that lead them to decide there are other concerns they have that require them to define policy. Should you have those five areas covered, you have the basics of governance and you can then move on to address other areas.

MBC: If I'm a dentist, what's involved in my answering each of the questions that you just posed?

Art: When we work with dentists, we always give them our thoughts about answers, but we always say, "You know, this is your practice. You get to decide what's right for you or what works for you and your partners in the marketplace that you're working in."

The bottom line of what's involved in answering each question is some very careful thought and open communication between the owners of the practice and any key advisors that they have. With careful thought and open communication, you can almost always create good, sound policies that you can then use as a basis for rolling forward.

I think this is a good time to say this! Policies are written on paper and they serve the practice so they can be changed. Policy-setting is an ongoing, evolutionary process. Part of it is developing the discipline and skill to stick with governance. You are governing your practice into the future – not just sitting down at one point in time, writing out some answers to questions and then going back to things the way you did them.

MBC: Why is a written vision and values statement critically important?

Art: "Vision" too often ends up being just way-up-in-the-sky generalities. But we take a very pragmatic approach. We want to know how you, as the owner of your practice, define "success" two, three, four or five years out – in terms of the size of the practice, the number of partners, the services offered, the revenues it will generate and the compensation you want to receive. That's necessary for you to have a very clear view when you get there of whether you have achieved the success you want.

In the same vein, what are the standards and principles that you will use to guide key decisions? We know dentists have taken "values" seriously when they start telling stories about how an issue has come up. Maybe it's an employee concern or maybe it's a patient concern. They can tell you the story about how they went back to their values and used them to answer their question.

When you write down your vision for the future and your values for how you will make decisions, it shows that you are serious enough to use them in making decisions in your practice. When you're serious about it, it's much more likely that you'll get there. That's a law of human behavior, not just a law of governance.

MBC: Many partners meet on a monthly basis to discuss practice problems and make decisions that need to be made. Is that what you mean by governance?

Art: It may be the first evolutionary stage of governance. I never want to say that there isn't such a thing as informal hallway governance that occurs. For us, the acid test is whether you have answered the five questions of ownership. Are you clear about your vision and values? Are you clear about the benefits that you want? Do you know how you're going to make key decisions about your practice, particularly when it gets stressful? Do you know who's going to manage the practice, what that person is expected to accomplish and what authority he or she has?

In that monthly process, you can come up with answers to those questions and write them down in some form. When you then use those answers to the questions to lead and manage your practice, it may take very little for you to put in what we would call an effective governance program.

I think the bottom line question is whether the process, if it's covering the five questions, is working efficiently and effectively for you. One of the things we hear a lot from dentists is that it seems to take way too long to deal with issues. They tell us their time is so constrained right now that they need to be able to process everything – from long-term, important decisions to daily problems – more efficiently and effectively.

I'm going to bet that the monthly informal or semi-formal meeting is taking way more time and energy than you need it to.

MBC: That's interesting. One of our clients today is in anguish over whether to retain an employee or let her go. She had been gone for a period of time and while she was gone the practice functioned very well without her. When she returned, they weren't sure what to do with her. I asked the simple question, "What's your policy?" Clearly, they had no answer for that and that demonstrates right there the importance of policy. Had the practice had one, coming to that conclusion wouldn't have been such an effort.

Art: I suspect, knowing you and how you work with your practices, that they at least had some values to fall back on. But you're right about having some policies to supplement the values.

MBC: It would have been remarkable if they had said, "Well, our policy is..." The policy then decides – and not their emotions. That's what they're in the middle of. Most practices have an office manager. What more do they need to do to define the things that they call "management"?

Art: It's answering Questions 4 and 5. Does that manager have clearly defined objectives and outcomes that he or she is responsible for? Does he or she have clearly defined authority for where he or she can take action or not take action without checking with the partners?

Is there a clearly defined relationship to the owners, so that he or she knows how and when to discuss issues with them – and is it clear what kinds of issues merit discussion with the partners?

If those are well-defined and written down, you've got Questions 4 and 5 of governance handled well. Most practices don't. Many have written down policies, but they have not clearly defined what they hold people accountable for and what levels of authority they will give them. So it all ends up coming back to the owner to manage the practice.

MBC: How about if a practice doesn't feel like it needs a manager or administrator? Are you saying that it does need one?

Art: No. What we're saying is the owners need to decide how they will manage. Remember our perspective is that if you don't pay attention to governance, management and doing the work will crowd governance out.

In a system where you're saying, "We don't want a manager-administrator," it's very useful to decide that one of the partners who has an interest in management becomes the managing partner. That person would then take accountability for day-to-day management of the practice and report back to the owners about it.

That would then allow you to charge that managing partner with accomplishing the objectives for the month or year that will get you to the benefits you want and help you achieve your vision for the future of the practice.

You may decide you don't want a managing partner. Then it becomes very important for the owners to say, "We don't want an administrator, a manager or a managing partner. So how are we going to manage in a way that's effective and makes the best use of our time?" That's the key question of governance.

MBC: What if my staff knows its jobs and knows the limits to its authority? What use is it to write down what everybody already knows?

Art: How do you know they know? If it's not written down, and it's just sort of "out there," you may think they know, they may think they know, but you may actually have different definitions that you're working on.

What happens is when there's a serious problem or breakdown, you wind up discovering under duress that what you thought everybody knew they didn't actually know.

I'm going to bet that a practice where nothing is written down and where everything is left sort of out in the atmosphere has dentists who wind up managing many, many, many detailed issues. That is because the staff generally will take those issues to the dentists for decisions. That pulls them away from the helm of the practice and down onto the deck, swabbing floors and setting sails.

MBC: What is a policy and why must it be written?

Art: It's useful to think of a policy as nothing more than a decision. It's a big decision that guides or constrains many other decisions. For example, if you set a policy that any staff person can make an adjustment of up to $50 on a patient complaint, all of a sudden you've guided and constrained many, many decisions day in, day out in your practice. That's very different from making a decision to adjust my bill by $50. The latter is a decision, not a policy. Policy is a decision that guides and constrains many other decisions.

Why must it be written? So that you consistently apply the policy over time. Memory is very poor under pressure, particularly in situations where emotions are high or there's conflict. Having written policies allows you to manage through those situations and not rely solely on relationships, memory and emotion.

MBC: Won't that create a lot of bureaucracy for small dental practices?

Art: What you need to look at in answering that is the cost of your current bureaucracy. I think in a practice without a good governance structure, you generally have lengthy non-productive meetings, confused roles for the partners and the managers, difficulties between partners, maybe failed partnerships, lost opportunities, poor decision-making and conflict.

All of that takes additional time and energy from you, the dentist owner, and from your staff. That is what I call the costs of hidden bureaucracy. You're right. A governance structure is substituting a visible bureaucracy that can be managed for a hidden bureaucracy that really can't be managed or isn't managed very well. You can make it more effective so that it takes less of your time and energy.

MBC: Let's say I'm convinced that my partners and I want a practice where policy governs. How do I get started?

Art: I would engage your partners and lead staff in the need for clarity on the five questions of ownership. You need cooperation from your partners and your lead staff.

Go through that with them and really communicate to them how you see the practice being different and better by taking on the governance challenge. I think that is the very first step.

Then, organize a series of meetings to address each of the five questions. Frankly, the order we presented them in in this discussion makes a lot of sense. But just know they are all connected to each other. I don't know that we would say you have to do them in a certain order, but we would suggest you follow that type of format.

You want to write down your answers in a form that is easily understood and retrieved – and keep them simple. Have a meeting at least quarterly to review your policies and performance on the year's objectives. You can then create new written policies to address problem areas or concerns as they come up or where you see that structured policies will help you address them.

Annually review your vision, values and policies. We suggest a strategic planning meeting of at least a day and a half. At that annual meeting, review your vision, values, policies and performance toward your objectives. Set objectives for the next year based on any changes in the vision, values and policies you see necessary.

If you keep the quarterly and annual cycles moving and reserve time to answer the governance questions about where your practice is going – What's our vision? What are our values and policies that we will use to get us there? – you will keep your governance process rolling forward and meeting the needs of your practice.

MBC: How does having those structures in place increase the assets, or negotiable value, of my practice?

Art: When you ask that question you're assuming that enhanced assets or increased negotiable value is one of the benefits you want from your practice. Just by stating that you want to increase the negotiable value you're saying that's part of your vision for the future. Getting that down specifically is part of the vision. The next question is to what level? How much do you want to increase it?

MBC: A zillion dollars.

Art: That's not a vision. That's a dream. Interestingly enough, though, it's one of the things we often hear from practices we work with. "Well, I want it to increase," they say. But you can't manage that. We always ask, "You want it to increase from what to what – and based on what measurement?"

MBC: Like any business owner, I want a return on my investment and I would like it to be as dramatic as possible. At some point, I would like to sell the asset either through partnership over time or to a buyer.

Art: You ask the question, "How can governance make that happen?" It's by making that wish explicit and by starting then to map out a pathway for how to get from here to there in annual increments. You go from what you'd like to have happen in the future to what you're going to do to make it happen.

When most dentists confront the issue of negotiable value, it drives them to bringing on additional partners. It's through the partnership renewal of the practice that the older dentists are able to cash out the asset value as the newer partners join in. As I think we've said a number of times here, answering the five questions of governance as a partner group very much increases the likelihood of success of the strategy of bringing in new partners and growing the practice so the negotiable asset value increases.

MBC: The thing I often find with our work is when you employ a governance structure and decisions are made through governance and not through personality, prospective buyers see that reproducibility – the reliability and the consistency of decision-making – is much higher and that decisions are less arbitrary and capricious.

That, in itself, increases the opportunity and the ability to do business, which increases the asset value. How difficult is it to implement a governance program in a dental practice? What's your experience there?

Art: It really does depend on whether you have good, sound communication skills and a high degree of pre-existing alignment around the vision for the future and the core values of your practice, not to mention a pretty good track record of making decisions in an efficient and effective manner.

That can be relatively easy – and maybe even enjoyable. What we find with many practices in that category is it's really putting voice and shape to ideas that have sort of been floating around amongst the partners. It makes those ideas specific and allows the partners to move forward on them more effectively.

For practices with a history of conflict and misalignment, either between the partners and the staff or among the partners or among everybody, doing that will take some work and some skill development. But I think if the desire is to take the helm of the practice and move the business forward, the rewards of developing the skills and competencies needed to make it happen can be very high.

MBC: Your process takes, what, five or six months for a fairly stable practice?

Art: It takes five or six months of about three hours a month, 90 minutes with us and 90 minutes of the group working independently. That's the advantage of the five questions of governance. You can walk through them in an orderly fashion so that each section builds on the last – so you come up with a good, solid base at the end of the process.

MBC: Where do you think the pitfalls will be in implementation of this? Dentists, like others, start with great enthusiasm and excitement about something. Then, over time, the day-to-day operations become kind of a dead end road until the enthusiasm disappears.

Art: I think there are three pitfalls that sort of depend upon the personality of the partners. One is you're all of a sudden making so many things explicit that it seems like there are so many issues you have to get on the table – governance issues and management issues – that you don't have plain old "meeting management" anymore.

That's the ability to put together a 90-minute meeting that moves through a variety of issues in an expeditious way so that the promise of a more efficient structure for management and governance doesn't seem so very far in the distance. Often it's just lack of good meeting management skills and not necessarily that anybody's doing anything wrong.

The second pitfall is falling back into overemphasizing management in the day-to-day work and not having the discipline to keep the vision, values and policy issues on the table – and then failing to use your written policies, so that you just fall back on old habits. It requires some discipline to develop new habits so that governance becomes the way you manage the practice. It takes some shifting of old habits.

The third pitfall -- and while I think it affects a minority of dentists, it's certainly there -- is actually going the other way and paying too much attention to the big blue sky vision and values. You then don't get down to the hard work of what to create in five years in concrete terms.

When you focus exclusively on "What are we going to hold our management accountable for this month and this year?" you can get sort of theoretical and you can lose sight of what needs to be done to produce results day in and day out.

I think in broad terms these would be the three potential pitfalls.

MBC: Thanks Art, I think people will have a much better
        understanding of this entire domain of governance.

CONCLUSION

Partnership is a human invention. You can't feel it, smell it, taste it or hear it. A partnership is not tangible, measurable or even directly observable. There is no such "thing" as a partnership. It is something that human beings have created to represent a number of perceived occurrences, relationships, activities and outcomes. It's simply a way we interpret the world. Therefore, partnership is a context, and as I have always said, "context is decisive."

One intention of this book has been to provide you with a new way of thinking about partnership and therefore alter your context of partnership. If you now think about partnership differently than before you read this book, it has accomplished its mission.

A well-designed and well-managed partnership is far more than the sum of its parts. It can generate synergy such that the financial and clinical outcomes are far greater than could be accomplished alone. A good partnership can infuse well-being, joy and satisfaction into your career. A dental partnership that really works is simply more effective, more productive and more enlivening than practicing alone.

But the fact remains that dentists often make lousy partners. That is a product of their training, their culture and their personality types. But it doesn't have to be this way. And that is what this book intended for you to see – along with giving you information and insights on how to make your current and future associateships and partnerships work.

And speaking of work, partnerships do not sustain themselves without constant vigilance and input. There is no "cruise control" to maintain the health of a partnership. If you are going to have a partnership, you'd better come to grips with the fact it is going to require you to work on it until you retire or leave the practice. But the rewards of a partnership in terms of free time, money, camaraderie, contribution and well-being are certainly worth it.

My recommendation is that you have your associate or partner read this book. Then spend some time discussing the various pieces of information presented. Share insights you and your associate or partner have uncovered about yourselves or about the partnership itself.

I suggest you follow the advice in this book, given what's at stake, what you have to lose and what you have to gain. Using the recommendations in this book will ensure that your future or current partnership prospers and lasts.

Dr. Marc Cooper

President, The Mastery Company
mcooper@MasteryCompany.com
MasteryCompany.com

Dr. Cooper is President and CEO of The Mastery Company. He has been a consultant to the health care industry for nearly 25 years – at the practice management level as well as at corporate and organizational levels. Prior to his consulting career, Dr. Cooper was an academician, basic science researcher and practicing periodontist.

His consulting clients have included more than 2,000 dentists practicing in solo, partnered and group practices and their corresponding support staffs. Dr. Cooper has also worked with senior executives, managers and supervisors in large health care systems, regional and community hospitals, third-party payers, clearinghouses, biotechnical firms, information technology companies, IPAs, PPOs, DPMs and DHMOs.

Dr. Cooper focuses the majority of his work on dentists in private practice, training and coaching them to achieve mastery as leaders, managers and owners who are able to consistently operate their dental practices as successful businesses.

ORDER FORM

Fax: (603) 720-0369. Send completed form.

Telephone: Call (425) 806-8830. Have your credit card ready.

Postal: Sahalie Press, PO Box 1806, Woodinville, WA 98072

Online: http://www.amazon.com

I understand that I may return any item for a full refund – for any reason, no questions asked.

☐   Mastering the Business of Practice ($19.95)
☐   Partnership: Why Some Succeed, Why Some Fail ($14.95)
☐   SOURCE: The Genesis of Success in Business & Life ($11.95)
☐   Running on Empty; Answers to Questions Dentists have about the Recession ($11.95)
☐   Subscription to the Mastery Newsletter (FREE)

Name_____

Shipping Address _____

_____

City_____   State _____   Zip Code _____

Sales Tax: Add 8.9% sales tax for products shipped to Washington addresses.

Shipping by Air:

U.S. $5.00 for first book/disk and $2.00 for each additional product.

Payment: ☐   Personal Check
             ☐   Credit Card (Visa, MasterCard or Amex)

Card Number:_____   Exp_____

Name on Card: _____

Billing Address if different from Shipping Address above.

_____

_____

DEDICATION

To Ami Pan Cooper

Daughter, Inspiration and Challenger

Made in the USA
Middletown, DE
07 December 2016